FOLLOW THE MONEY WITH NEW MEXICO PUBLIC RECORDS

A 505 LEGAL GUIDE

KENNETH H. STALTER

Published by Stalter Law LLC
PO Box 90336, Albuquerque, NM 87199
www.505legal.com

Library of Congress Cataloging-in-Publication Data
Stalter, Kenneth H.
Follow the Money with New Mexico Public Records: A 505 Legal Guide / Kenneth H. Stalter
ISBN: 979-8-9928381-1-4

Printed in the United States of America
First Edition: 2026

CONTENTS

ABOUT 505 LEGAL

505 Legal is the modern hometown law firm for New Mexico, built for moments when life collides with the legal system.

We combine trial-ready advocacy with modern tools, clear advice, and a deep commitment to the communities we serve. Grounded, decisive, and prepared to take cases to resolution—by negotiation or in court—505 Legal exists to cut through fear and confusion and help people move forward when it matters most.

Publishing practical legal guides is part of that mission. By explaining the law in clear, plain English, we aim to demystify a system that too often feels opaque and intimidating. These guides are not a substitute for representation—they are an extension of it—helping people understand their options, ask better questions, and approach legal problems with confidence rather than panic.

ABOUT THE AUTHOR

Kenneth H. Stalter was born in Albuquerque and returned to New Mexico after graduating from Harvard Law School. He has worked on both sides of the courtroom—as a prosecutor handling felony trials, as general counsel for the New Mexico Attorney General's Office, and now as co-founder of 505 Legal.

His current practice focuses on civil litigation ranging from injury and insurance claims to civil rights and government accountability. He has brought multiple successful IPRA enforcement actions against state agencies, including cases that changed how those agencies handle public records requests.

He wrote this book because he believes transparency is too important to leave to lawyers. Every New Mexican has the right to know how their government spends public money. This guide is designed to help you exercise that right.

DISCLAIMER

This book teaches you about New Mexico's public records law. It is not legal advice for your situation.

Laws change. Courts read them differently over time. Details like a missed deadline can change everything. What worked for someone else might not work for you.

Reading this book does not make me your lawyer. If you think an agency violated your rights, talk to an attorney who can look at your specific facts.

Use this book to learn how IPRA works and what questions to ask. But when it comes to your case, get real legal help. A good place to start would be 505 Legal, PC at www.505legal.com. Please see Part 9 of this book for more information about contacting our firm.

INTRODUCTION
YOUR RIGHT TO FOLLOW THE MONEY

In New Mexico, the government uses tax dollars to pay for things like school buildings, road repairs, water systems, and police departments. But who makes sure this money gets spent wisely?

Often, that job falls to citizens like you.

The Inspection of Public Records Act—IPRA—puts real power in your hands. It's not just a law on the books. It's a practical tool that lets you see what your government does with your money.

What IPRA Does

You already have ways to track government spending. Those ways include public meetings, agency websites, legal notices, and public databases. But these tools share one limitation: you only see what the government chooses to show you.

IPRA is different. Under this law, you have the right to see records the government holds—even records it hasn't made public. The catch? You have to ask.

When you submit a proper request, the agency must respond. They have fifteen days to either give you the records or explain why they won't. If they violate the law, you can sue—and potentially win monetary damages.

What counts as a "public record"? Almost everything: documents, emails, letters, maps, photographs, recordings, contracts, and more. If a government office created or received a document, you can probably request that document.

What IPRA Doesn't Cover

IPRA applies to New Mexico state and local government, from the Governor's Office down to your local water and sanitation district.

IPRA does not apply to the federal government. A different law, the Freedom of Information Act (FOIA), covers federal records requests. I've included FOIA resources in Appendix III, but this book focuses on New Mexico law.

Where to Find IPRA

The law itself appears at Chapter 14, Article 2, Sections 1 through 12 of the New Mexico Statutes. You can read it at www.nmonesource. com. Here's a direct link to IPRA:

https://nmonesource.com/nmos/nmsa/en/item/4383/index.do

I've also included the full text in Appendix I. But laws change, so always check the official version before relying on it.

The Gap Between Rights and Results

There's a big difference between knowing you have the right to request records and knowing how to do so effectively.

Random, overly broad requests—"give me all contracts" or "show me all spending"—rarely work. Agencies get overwhelmed. Responses get delayed. And if you get an answer at all, you may end up with thousands of pages that don't tell you what you need to know.

This guide shows you a better approach. You'll learn how to:

- Focus your requests on specific projects or vendors
- Use publicly available information to frame targeted questions
- Understand contract documents when you get them
- Spot patterns that might signal problems
- Take effective action when you find issues

IPRA gives you the legal right. This book teaches you the strategy to use it well.

Meet Maria

Throughout this guide, you'll follow Maria as she learns to use IPRA. Maria is fictional, but her story combines the real experiences of New Mexicans I've helped through my law firm.

Maria is 34, a mother of three, and a part-time nursing assistant in a city in northern New Mexico. She's not a lawyer or journalist. She's a regular person who got fed up with how her city spends money.

It started when construction began on a big development near her neighborhood. The project seemed to appear overnight. Rumors spread about the mayor's ties to the developer. Maria went to a city council meeting and asked questions. She got vague answers about "proper procedures." Without documents to back her up, officials dismissed her and moved on.

This happened again and again. Maria showed up with real concerns. Officials treated her like a crank. She knew something was wrong, but she couldn't prove it.

Then she learned about IPRA. At first, she thought it was only for reporters or lawyers. She was wrong. As you'll see, any citizen can use this law.

This guide follows Maria's journey. You'll watch her request records, hit roadblocks, figure out what she's reading, and take action. Her story shows how the strategies in each chapter work in real life—even if you have no special training.

PART 1

UNDERSTANDING YOUR RIGHTS

What IPRA Is and How It Works

New Mexico's Inspection of Public Records Act gives you the right to see government records. Any person can request records from any state or local agency. You don't need to explain why you want them. You don't need a lawyer. You just need to ask in writing.

The Basic Idea

Government works for you. You pay for it. You have a right to see what it does with your money and in your name.

The idea behind IPRA is simple: all government records are open unless a specific exception applies. The government must justify withholding records. You don't have to justify asking for them.

Who Must Respond

Every state and local government agency must follow IPRA:

- State agencies and departments
- Cities and counties
- School districts
- Police and sheriff's departments
- Special districts (water, sewer, fire)
- Public universities and colleges
- Boards and commissions

If a private company is doing work for the government, that company may have to produce records related to that work.

What Counts as a Public Record

IPRA defines public records broadly. Public records include any document—paper or electronic—that a government agency creates, receives, or maintains. This includes:

- Emails and text messages
- Contracts and invoices
- Meeting minutes
- Policies and procedures
- Reports and studies
- Personnel records (with some limits)
- Body camera footage
- Spending records

Format doesn't matter. Paper files, databases, videos, and audio recordings are all public records if they relate to government business.

How to Make a Request

Put your request in writing. Email works. So does a letter or fax. Include:

1. Your name, address, and phone number
2. A description of the records you want

That's it. No special forms. No need to cite the law. Just be clear about what you're asking for.

The Timeline

Once an agency receives your written request, the clock starts. Here's what should happen and when.

Three Business Days: The Acknowledgment

Within three business days, the agency must do one of two things:

1. Give you the records, or
2. Send you a written response explaining when you'll get them

This first response is sometimes called a "three-day letter." It doesn't have to include records—just confirmation that your request was received and a target date for completion.

Business days don't include weekends or state holidays. If you submit a request on Thursday, the agency has until the following Tuesday to acknowledge it (assuming no holidays).

What if you hear nothing? Silence within three days isn't a violation by itself. But it's a warning sign. Send a polite follow-up:

> I submitted a records request on [date]. Please confirm receipt and provide an estimated completion date.

Fifteen Calendar Days: Records or Denial

The agency has fifteen calendar days to either:

1. Let you inspect the records, or
2. Explain in writing why it's denying your request

Calendar days means every day counts—weekends included. If you submit a request on June 1st, the deadline is June 16th.

A proper denial must cite specific legal reasons. "These records are confidential" isn't good enough. The agency must point to a specific IPRA exception or another law that allows withholding.

If day fifteen passes with no records and no explanation, you can treat your request as denied. At that point, you have the right to sue.

When Requests Take Longer: The "Burdensome" Exception

Some requests legitimately need more time. If your request covers thousands of pages or requires searching multiple departments, the agency can invoke the "excessively burdensome or broad" exception.

When this happens, the agency must:

- Notify you in writing within fifteen days that extra time is needed
- Complete the request within a "reasonable" time

The law doesn't define "reasonable." That frustrates everyone. Here's how I think about it:

- A few specific documents => 15 days (the standard deadline)
- Hundreds of documents => 30 to 60 days
- Thousands of documents => 60 to 90 days

In my opinion, all IPRA requests (even the most complex) should be completed in 90 days. These aren't legal rules—they're practical benchmarks based on what courts and requesters generally accept. A 3,000-page request isn't getting done in fifteen days. But it shouldn't take two years either.

But reasonable timeframes aren't just about volume. A single, specific document—like one report on an identified topic—might run hundreds of pages. That's still one document the agency should be able to locate and produce within the standard fifteen days. What takes time is searching across departments, gathering records from multiple sources, and reviewing large numbers of files for redactions.

What "Reasonable" Depends On

Several factors affect what counts as reasonable:

- **Volume:** More pages means more time. That's fair.
- **Complexity:** Records scattered across departments take longer to gather than files in one place.
- **Redaction needs:** If records contain exempt information (like Social Security numbers or attorney-client communications), someone must review and redact before release. That adds time.
- **Agency resources:** A small water district with one part-time clerk can't move as fast as a state agency with dedicated staff.

What's not a good excuse:

- "We're busy with other things." IPRA compliance is part of the job.
- "We don't want to release this." The law doesn't care what they want.
- "Our staff doesn't know how to search for these records." That's their problem to solve.

Following Up During Long Waits

For requests that stretch beyond fifteen days, stay engaged. Send status updates every two to four weeks:

> I'm following up on my records request dated [date]. Please provide an update on the current status and estimated completion date.

Keep it short. Keep it professional. Document every exchange.

If months pass with no progress, push harder. Ask for a specific completion date. Ask what's causing the delay. Put the agency on notice that you're tracking their response time carefully.

Rolling Productions

For large requests, ask the agency to produce records in batches as they become available. This is called a "rolling production."

Instead of waiting six months for everything, you might receive:

- Month 1: Emails from the project manager

- Month 2: Contracts and invoices
- Month 3: Meeting minutes and memos

This approach benefits everyone. You get useful information sooner. The agency spreads out the workload. And the ongoing production shows they're actually working on your request.

What It Costs

Inspecting records is free. You can visit the agency's office and look at documents without paying anything.

If you want copies:

- **Paper copies:** Up to $1 per page
- **Electronic copies:** The agency can charge for the storage device (like a thumb drive) plus actual mailing costs
- **Staff time:** No charge for searching or reviewing records

Always ask for electronic copies. They're cheaper and easier to search.

What's Not Public

IPRA has exceptions. Some records are off-limits:

- Medical records
- Letters of reference in personnel files
- Opinions in personnel evaluations
- Trade secrets
- Attorney-client communications
- Certain law enforcement records during active investigations
- Personal information like Social Security numbers and home addresses of government employees

When an agency withholds records, it must tell you which exception applies. A blanket "no" isn't allowed.

When Agencies Don't Comply

If an agency ignores your request or wrongly denies it, you have options.

File a lawsuit. You can go to district court to force compliance. If you win, the agency pays your attorney fees and court costs.

Seek penalties. A court can order the agency to pay up to $100 per day for unreasonable delays or failures to respond.

Contact the Attorney General. The AG's office provides guidance on IPRA compliance and can bring enforcement actions.

The Bottom Line

IPRA is one of the strongest public records laws in the country. It assumes records are public. It puts deadlines on government. It makes agencies pay when they break the rules.

You don't need permission to ask questions. You don't need connections or credentials. You just need to know how to use the tool.

Why IPRA Works Well for Financial Oversight

The rest of this book focuses on using IPRA to examine government spending and contracts. IPRA is especially powerful in this area for two reasons.

Financial Records Get Strong Protection

Financial records go to the heart of government accountability. The public has a clear interest in knowing how public funds get spent.

Some information might be exempt—trade secrets, personal identifiers. But the core financial details are almost always public: who got paid, how much, and for what.

The Procurement Code Creates a Paper Trail

Most government spending happens under the New Mexico Procurement Code. This law sets the rules agencies must follow when buying goods and services. The Procurement Code typically covers things like a county hiring a contractor to build a bridge or a school district purchasing computers.

The law requires competition, fairness, and—most important for our purposes—documentation.

Agencies must create records at every stage:

- **Before buying:** What they need and why
- **During selection:** Bids received, evaluation scores, justifications for choices
- **After awarding:** Invoices, payment records, proof of delivery

This paper trail exists whether the purchase costs five thousand dollars or five million. These procurement records are public records under IPRA. You have the right to see them.

Understanding public funding means following the money. To follow the money, procurement documents are often your best source. Later chapters show you how to request and analyze these records.

Other Government Spending

Not all government money flows through the Procurement Code.

Exempt agencies. By law, some agencies and offices operate outside the Procurement Code entirely. But "exempt" doesn't mean "undocumented." These agencies typically have their own procurement policies requiring competitive bids, written justifications, and payment records. The paperwork looks similar—it just follows different rules. These records are still public under IPRA.

Payroll and benefits. Agencies spend heavily on employee salaries, benefits, and pensions. These costs follow different rules but still generate records. Payroll documents, position descriptions, salary schedules, and benefit plans are all public.

Grants. Governments distribute money through grants to nonprofits, local agencies, and other organizations. Grant programs create their own paper trails: applications, award letters, contracts, progress reports, and expenditure records.

The specific records vary by spending type. The principle stays the same: documentation should exist showing how much was spent and what the public received. IPRA gives you the right to see it.

What You Can Uncover

Government agencies don't always police themselves. Auditors are stretched thin. Reporters can't cover everything. Citizens like you often provide the accountability.

With IPRA, you can search for:

- **Inappropriate spending:** Purchases that don't make sense, costs that seem inflated, payments for work never done
- **Conflicts of interest:** Governmental officials giving contracts to relatives, personal associates, or campaign donors
- **Anti-donation violations:** The New Mexico Constitution includes an "anti-donation" clause. This clause says that the government usually cannot give money or resources to private parties without getting equal value in return
- **Fraud:** Contractors who made promises to win government money but never delivered

The records exist. IPRA gives you the key.

Maria's Journey: Understanding Your Rights

Maria was fed up. Another council meeting, another runaround. Officials glossed over her questions about the development contract. She left feeling powerless—again.

Her neighbor Joseph had a suggestion. "You don't need to take their word for it. You have a right to see those contracts."

"Isn't that just for reporters?" Maria asked.

"No. I used it last year to get records about the water system. The law says 'every person' can inspect public records. That means you."

That night, Maria looked up IPRA. What she found surprised her.

She didn't need a lawyer. She didn't need to explain why she wanted the records. She just had to ask in writing.

Better yet, the city couldn't ignore her. They had three business days to acknowledge her request. They had 15 days to hand over records or explain why not. If they blew the deadline, she could take them to court.

Maria also stumbled across the Procurement Code—over a hundred sections of rules about government purchasing. "I'll never understand all this," she thought.

Then she remembered Joseph's advice: "You don't need to master the code. You just need to know what records should exist."

She opened an AI tool and typed: "What records should exist if a city followed the Procurement Code when awarding a development contract?"

The answer gave her a list:

- The request for proposals
- All bids submitted—including losers
- The winning contract
- Emails about the project
- Meeting minutes where it was discussed
- Any amendments to the deal
- Payment records

She also learned something important: if the city refused to release a record, they had to say exactly why. "It's confidential" wasn't good enough. They had to cite a specific legal exemption.

Maria felt something shift. She wasn't begging anymore. She had rights. The city had obligations. And if they didn't comply, she had options.

She started drafting her first request.

PART 2

BEFORE YOU MAKE YOUR FIRST REQUEST

Do Your Homework First

The best IPRA requests don't start with IPRA. They start with research.

Before you ask for records, spend time learning what's already public. This groundwork focuses your requests and helps you understand what you find later.

Where to Find Public Spending Information

New Mexico governments put significant financial information online. Here's where to look:

- **Agency websites:** Most agencies post budgets, financial reports, and procurement policies
- **Meeting agendas and minutes:** Look for items labeled "contract approval" or "expenditure authorization"

- **Public notices:** Legally required announcements about requests for proposals (RFPs)
- **Open data portals:** Some larger governments publish searchable spending data
- **Sunshine Portal:** The state's transparency website lists financial information for state agencies
- **Audits and reports:** The State Auditor posts audits of state and local agencies online. The Legislative Finance Committee publishes detailed fiscal analyses

Appendix IV includes a list of key public databases and transparency portals in New Mexico.

What to Look For

As you review these sources, watch for details that will sharpen your IPRA requests:

- Project names and descriptions
- Contract or purchase order numbers
- RFP numbers and identifiers
- Dollar amounts and approval dates
- Vendor names
- Which department handles the project
- Names of staff analysts, evaluation committee members, and contract signers
- References to authorizing resolutions or legislation
- Related agenda items from public meetings

This information becomes valuable when you craft your request.

Stay Organized from the Start

Save documents. Take screenshots. Keep detailed notes. Record where you found each piece of information.

If you start organizing your information early, you are more likely to have a clear picture later. You don't need fancy software—a basic spreadsheet works. Create columns for:

- Project name
- Agency or department
- Date approved
- Contract amount
- Vendor name
- Contract number
- Source of information
- Notes and concerns

This system helps you spot patterns and keeps your investigation focused.

Two Research Tips

Use site-specific searches. Government websites don't always make documents easy to find. Sometimes the document you need exists on the website but isn't linked from any main page. Google lets you search within a single website by typing site: followed by the web address, then your search terms.

For example, to find documents about "water treatment" on Bernalillo County's website, type into Google:

```
site:bernco.gov water treatment contract
```

This often uncovers documents you'd never find by clicking through menus.

Look beyond the decision-makers. Elected officials and agency heads have final authority, but staff do the real work. A commissioner might vote on a contract based on a one-page summary. The analyst who prepared that summary has emails, spreadsheets, and draft reports showing the full picture.

When a meeting agenda lists a staff presenter, that person's files often reveal more than the commission members' files. Target your requests accordingly.

Identifying What to Target

Not all government spending deserves the same scrutiny. Focus on:

- **Outliers:** Projects that cost far more than similar past efforts
- **Patterns:** The same vendors winning contracts repeatedly, especially without competitive bidding
- **Timing:** Contracts approved unusually fast or during holiday periods when oversight is light
- **Connections:** Vendors with potential ties to decision-makers
- **Public concerns:** Projects that generated community complaints or news coverage

If something feels off but you can't pinpoint why, try describing the facts to an AI tool like ChatGPT or Claude. It can help you identify patterns or articulate what seems wrong.

The Mental Game

Patience matters. Expect roadblocks. Expect to spend time organizing and understanding what you receive. No one will hand you answers on a silver platter.

Don't give up. Accountability is a long game. This book exists to help you stay in it.

Maria's Journey: Doing the Homework

Maria wanted to fire off her first request right away. But Joseph's words stuck with her: "Do some homework first. It'll save you weeks."

That night, after the kids were in bed, she sat at her kitchen table with her laptop. She poked around the city's website and found a "Transparency Portal" buried at the bottom of the homepage.

She clicked through PDFs of council agendas and minutes. She found the meeting where the development got approved. The minutes were thin—just one line: "Council approved the Main Street development agreement with Sundagger Ventures LLC." But they included a resolution number: 2023-42.

Maria wrote it down. She kept digging.

Under "Awarded Contracts," she found more. Sundagger Ventures had a $4.2 million contract for "infrastructure development." Contract number: CON-2023-0422. Approved three months ago.

Then she searched the company name. Sundagger had received three other city contracts in the past two years. That seemed odd for a company she'd never heard of.

Maria opened a spreadsheet and made columns: project name, contract number, date, amount, notes. She filled in what she knew. She flagged what was missing.

She also noticed a reference to "Campaign Contribution Disclosure Statements" that contractors had to file. Were Sundagger's owners donors to local officials? She added those forms to her list.

By the end of the night, Maria had traded vague suspicions for specific targets:

- Contract CON-2023-0422
- Resolution 2023-42
- The Request for Proposals
- Scoring sheets from the bid evaluation
- Ownership documents for Sundagger Ventures
- Campaign contribution disclosures from Sundagger or its owners

She wasn't going to ask for "all information about the development" anymore. She had contract numbers, resolution numbers, and company names. She had a real list.

Her kitchen-table homework had taken two hours. It would save her weeks.

PART 3

CRAFTING EFFECTIVE REQUESTS

Why Specific Requests Win

The difference between getting records and hitting a wall often comes down to how you write your request. IPRA requires you to identify the records you want with "reasonable particularity." Vague requests create problems for everyone.

Think about it from the agency's perspective. If you ask for "all information about county spending," you might be asking for ten thousand documents from a dozen different offices. A clerk that receives that request would have good reason to delay or even deny the request.

Specific requests:

- Get processed faster
- Are harder for agencies to sidestep
- Produce more relevant information
- Are easier to enforce if denied

There's a practical benefit too: if you care about one project, you don't want to wade through thousands of pages about other projects.

The Elements of an Effective Request

A good request for contract or spending records includes:

1. **Precise identification:** Contract numbers, project names, or vendor names
2. **Clear time period:** Specific date ranges—not "the past several years"
3. **Document types:** The exact categories of records you want
4. **Department information:** Which part of the agency holds these records
5. **Format preference:** Electronic or paper (choose electronic when possible)

Sample Request Language

Here's how to structure requests for different financial records:

For a specific contract:

I request:

The full contract between [Agency] and [Vendor] for [Project Name] (Contract #ABC-123) approved on [Date]

All amendments, change orders, or modifications to this contract

All invoices submitted by [Vendor] under this contract

All payment records showing amounts paid to [Vendor] under this contract

For vendor performance:

> I request:
>
> All performance evaluations, inspection reports, or compliance documents related to [Vendor]'s work on [Project] from [Date] to [Date]
>
> Any notices of non-compliance or corrective action plans issued to [Vendor] regarding this project
>
> Any correspondence between project managers and [Vendor] addressing performance concerns

For procurement records:

> I request:
>
> The Request for Proposals (RFP #XYZ) for [Project]
>
> All submissions received in response to this RFP
>
> The scoring sheets or evaluation documents used to select the winning bidder
>
> The final selection memo or documentation justifying the contract award

Where to Submit Your Request

IPRA requires every agency to post instructions for submitting records requests. Look for this information on the agency's website—usually under headings like "Public Records," "IPRA Requests," or "Transparency."

Each agency handles requests differently:

- **Online portals:** Many larger agencies use systems like NextRequest or GovQA. You create an account, submit requests through the portal, and track responses online.
- **Email:** Some agencies accept requests by email to a designated address or records custodian.
- **Mail or fax:** Still accepted everywhere, though slower than electronic options.
- **In person:** You can hand-deliver a written request to the agency's office.

If you can't find submission instructions, call the agency's main number and ask for the records custodian. That's the person responsible for handling IPRA requests.

Document Everything

This matters: keep proof that you submitted your request. Take screenshots of online submissions. Save sent emails. If you mail a request, use certified mail with return receipt. If you hand-deliver a request, ask for a stamped copy for your records.

Why? If a dispute arises later, you may need to prove when you submitted your request and what you asked for. Agencies occasionally claim they never received a request. Documentation protects you.

Common Pitfalls to Avoid

Even well-intentioned requests go wrong. Here's how to avoid common mistakes:

Don't ask questions. "How much did the county spend on road repairs?" isn't a records request—it asks the agency to research and compile an answer. Instead, request "payment records for road repair projects from January through December 2023."

Avoid standalone "all." "All emails about the construction project" is too broad. Try instead: "Emails between the Project Manager and ABC Contractor regarding the Main Street Project from June through September 2023."

Don't mix unrelated topics. Combining requests for school bus contracts and police equipment makes it harder for the agency to respond. Submit separate requests for unrelated subjects.

Don't request records that don't exist. Agencies don't have to create documents or compile information for you. Request existing records only.

Real-World Example

Here's how these principles work in practice:

Weak request:

I want to see all information about the city's spending on consultants.

Strong request:

I request the following public records:

All contracts between the City of Las Cruces and ABC Consulting Group from January 1, 2022 to present

All invoices submitted by ABC Consulting Group under these contracts

All reports or deliverables produced by ABC Consulting Group under these contracts

Minutes from City Council meetings where these contracts were approved

I prefer to receive these records in electronic format.

The second request gives clear direction. The agency knows exactly what to look for. That makes it easier to fulfill—and harder to legitimately deny.

Maria's Journey: Writing the Request

Maria stared at a blank email. Her instinct was to vent—to pour out everything she suspected about Sundagger Ventures. Instead, she stuck to what she'd learned: be specific, not emotional.

She built a simple template:

Subject: Inspection of Public Records Act Request

To Whom It May Concern:

Under the New Mexico Inspection of Public Records Act, I request copies of the following public records:

[First record]

[Second record]

I prefer electronic copies. If you are not the custodian of these records, please forward this request to the proper custodian as required by law.

Then she filled in the specifics:

Contract CON-2023-0422 between the City and Sundagger Ventures LLC

All amendments or changes to that contract

Resolution 2023-42

The Request for Proposals that led to the contract

Bid evaluation and scoring sheets

Campaign Contribution Disclosure Statements filed by Sundagger Ventures or its owners since January 1, 2021

Joseph looked it over that night. "Good. But split it into two requests—contract documents in one, campaign contributions in the other. Harder for them to call it burdensome."

Maria sent the first request the next morning.

Three days later, she got an acknowledgment: the city had received her request and would respond within 15 days. A form letter, but proof they couldn't claim ignorance.

Day 14 came. Nothing. Then, that evening, an email: "Response to IPRA Request."

The city called it a "partial fulfillment." They sent the main contract and Resolution 2023-42. The rest would come "within a reasonable timeframe."

Maria was annoyed—but she had 48 pages she didn't have before. She read through the contract that night and spotted something: the document referenced "Exhibit C: Bid Evaluation Score Sheet." That exhibit wasn't attached.

The next morning, she followed up:

> Thank you for the partial response. The contract references "Exhibit C: Bid Evaluation Score Sheet," which was not included. Please provide this exhibit along with the remaining items.

Short. Polite. Specific.

Maria was getting the hang of this. Ask for exactly what you need. Follow up when pieces are missing. Keep pushing.

PART 4

UNDERSTANDING GOVERNMENT CONTRACTS

What You're Looking At

Government contracts contain dense language and technical terms. Don't let that intimidate you. Once you know what to look for, these documents tell a clear story about how public money gets spent.

A typical government contract includes:

- **Scope of work:** What the contractor must deliver
- **Payment terms:** How much they'll be paid and when
- **Timeline:** When the work should be completed
- **Performance standards:** How quality will be measured
- **Termination clauses:** When the contract can be ended

Each section reveals whether taxpayers are getting good value.

How Procurement Should Work

Before diving into specific contracts, understand how the process should function. It might be under the Procurement Code or an exempt agency's own policies. Either way, take the time to do your homework.

1. **Needs identification:** The agency determines what it needs
2. **Competitive procurement:** For larger purchases, the agency solicits multiple bids through a request for proposals (RFP)
3. **Evaluation:** Proposals are scored based on predetermined criteria
4. **Award:** The contract goes to the vendor offering the best value (not always the lowest price)
5. **Contract execution:** Terms are documented in a written agreement signed by both parties
6. **Contract management:** The agency monitors performance and authorizes payments

This process ensures fair competition and good value. Deviations often signal problems.

Red Flags: What to Watch For

When you review procurement documents, contracts, and payment records, you need to know what problems look like. Some red flags scream trouble. Others whisper. This section trains your eye to spot both.

Not every red flag means something illegal happened. Sometimes agencies cut corners because they're understaffed or rushing. Sometimes odd arrangements have good explanations. But red flags tell you where to look closer and when to keep digging.

Open Meetings Act Violations

Alongside IPRA, the Open Meetings Act (OMA) is one of New Mexico's flagship transparency laws. OMA is deserving of a book of its own, but for tracking government spending, you need to know one key principle: decisions about public money must happen in public view.

Watch for these warning signs when reviewing meeting minutes and agendas:

Failure to publish the agenda on time. OMA requires agencies to post meeting agendas at least 72 hours before regular meetings. When an agency approves a big contract at a meeting with no advance notice, ask yourself: did they want the public to show up?

Last-minute agenda changes or additions. A contract worth hundreds of thousands of dollars appears on the agenda the day before the vote. The public had no real chance to weigh in. This signals the decision was made somewhere else—and they're just going through the motions in public.

Rolling quorums. Three commissioners can't legally meet in private to decide how they'll vote. But what if Commissioner A meets with Commissioner B on Monday, then Commissioner B meets with Commissioner C on Tuesday? No single meeting had a quorum—but the majority reached consensus outside public view. Calendars and emails obtained through IPRA can reveal these patterns. Look for one-on-one meetings between board members in the days before a major spending vote, or email chains where members discuss the item separately rather than together.

Closed meetings or sessions. Governing bodies can close meetings for limited reasons—like discussing pending litigation or personnel matters. They cannot close meetings to discuss how to spend money. If minutes show a spending decision emerged from closed session, that's a red flag worth investigating.

When you spot these patterns through IPRA, you've found something worth digging into. The spending decision itself may be legal, but the process that led to it may not be.

Process Problems

Open Meetings issues are not the only process problems that arise.

The Procurement Code exists for a reason. Proper procedures keep prices fair and reduce favoritism. When agencies skip steps, problems follow.

No-bid contracts without justification. The law allows agencies to skip competitive bidding in limited cases—when only one vendor can do the work, or during genuine emergencies. But these exceptions get abused. Look for sole-source contracts that don't explain why competition wasn't possible. Could other companies have done this work? If yes, why didn't the agency let them compete?

Unusually short bidding periods. Agencies must give vendors enough time to prepare serious proposals. When a deadline falls just days after an RFP posts, insiders have an advantage. New competitors can't respond in time. Short windows may signal the agency already knows who it wants.

Limited advertising. The law requires agencies to publicize contracting opportunities. If an RFP appeared only on an obscure webpage for a few days, competition suffered. Limited advertising often means limited accountability.

Rushed approvals. Major contracts should get serious review. When a governing board approves a million-dollar deal with no discussion, no questions, and no dissent, something may be wrong. Check meeting minutes and videos. Did anyone ask hard questions? Did the approval happen on a consent agenda where items pass without individual votes?

Pre-selection signals. Sometimes RFP requirements are written so narrowly that only one vendor could qualify. These tailored specifications can be legitimate. They can also steer contracts to favored vendors while pretending to compete.

Split purchases. The Procurement Code sets dollar thresholds that trigger stricter requirements. Watch for agencies that split one purchase into several smaller ones to stay under the limit. If an agency bought the same equipment from the same vendor five times in one month, each purchase just under the threshold, that's a red flag.

Contract Term Problems

The contract itself shows what the agency agreed to pay for—and what protections it built in or failed to build in. Problems often hide in the details.

Vague deliverables. A good contract specifies exactly what the vendor must provide. A bad contract uses fuzzy language like "consulting services" or "program support" without definitions. Vague deliverables make it impossible to know whether the vendor performed.

Missing price breakdowns. When a contract shows only a lump sum, you can't tell if the price is reasonable. How much goes to labor? Materials? Profit? Without breakdowns, you can't compare to market rates or spot inflated costs.

No performance standards. Contracts should define success and consequences for falling short. Look for measurable benchmarks and reporting requirements. Without these protections, the agency gave away its leverage.

Payment before performance. Most contracts should tie payments to completed work. Large upfront payments create unnecessary risk. The vendor might underperform, disappear, or go bankrupt.

No verification requirements. Before paying invoices, agencies should verify work was done. Contracts should require documentation—inspection reports, delivery receipts, progress certifications. Without proof-of-performance requirements, the door opens for fraud.

Automatic renewals. Some contracts renew year after year without review. Others have no end date. These arrangements let relationships continue indefinitely without fresh competition. Prices creep up. The agency loses incentive to shop around.

Retroactive approvals. Work should not start before a contract is signed. A contract executed in March covering work done in January means someone jumped the gun. Retroactive approvals might mean the agency spent money without proper authorization.

Funding Problems

Legal government spending requires funds to be properly appropriated and actually available. Funding irregularities signal serious problems.

Unidentified funding sources. Every expenditure should trace to a specific budget line. If records don't show where money came from, ask why. Agencies sometimes hide questionable spending by keeping funding vague.

Wrong fund usage. Government money often comes with strings. If the law creating a tax limits how the money can be used, later projects must respect those limitations. Federal grants must be spent on approved purposes. When agencies tap restricted funds for unauthorized uses, they violate the law.

Spending beyond appropriations. Agencies can only spend money the legislature or governing board has appropriated. Watch for contracts that commit funds the agency doesn't legally have.

Grant timing violations. Grants have start and end dates. Expenses outside those dates aren't reimbursable. Watch for spending charged to grants before the grant period began or after it ended.

Relationship Problems

Government contracting should be impersonal. The best vendor wins, regardless of connections. But personal relationships corrupt the process.

Conflicts of interest. Decision-makers shouldn't have financial stakes in contracts they approve. Look for officials who vote on contracts with companies they own, invest in, or work for on the side.

Family connections. When contracts go to officials' relatives, questions arise. Family relationships don't automatically mean corruption, but they demand scrutiny. Was the process fair?

Former officials as vendors. People who leave government often sell back to their former agencies. They know the systems and the decision-makers. Watch for patterns—especially when former officials land contracts shortly after leaving.

Revolving door patterns. When agency officials leave to work for contractors they supervised, it raises questions. Did they steer contracts knowing a job waited on the other side?

Campaign contributor connections. When major donors receive major contracts, the appearance of corruption is hard to avoid. Cross-reference vendor names with campaign finance records.

Disclosure failures. New Mexico law requires officials to disclose financial interests and potential conflicts. Missing or incomplete disclosures may hide problematic relationships.

Performance Problems

Contracts are promises. When vendors don't keep theirs, taxpayers get cheated.

Work not performed. The simplest fraud: billing for work that never happened. Compare invoices to deliverables. Do the numbers add up? Does physical evidence exist?

Substandard quality. Some vendors deliver—but not what they promised. Construction that fails inspection. Reports full of errors. Equipment that breaks immediately. Check inspection records and complaint logs.

Persistent delays. When vendors consistently miss deadlines without consequence, there might be a problem.

Scope creep without authorization. Projects grow. But when scope expands significantly—and so does the price—proper procedures should apply. Were change orders approved in advance?

No performance documentation. Agencies should have records proving vendors performed before getting paid. If these records don't exist, how did anyone verify the work was done?

Ignored complaints. When users complain about a vendor's work and nothing changes, accountability has failed. Check whether problem vendors kept getting paid—and kept getting new contracts.

Timing Problems

Government budgeting follows cycles. When spending departs from normal timing, look closer.

Late fiscal year rushes. Agencies sometimes scramble to spend remaining budget before year-end, fearing they'll lose unspent funds. This leads to hasty purchases and corners cut. Heavy spending in the final weeks of a fiscal year deserves scrutiny.

Commitments before appropriation. Agencies can't legally spend money that hasn't been appropriated. Watch for contracts dated before the relevant budget was adopted.

Backdated paperwork. Purchase orders dated after purchases were made. Approvals signed after work began. Documentation created after auditors asked questions. Backdated paperwork signals deeper problems.

Vendor Representation Problems

Vendors make promises to win contracts. These promises aren't always true.

Credential misrepresentations. Proposals list certifications and licenses. Are they real? Verify through state licensing boards. A vendor claiming fake credentials has committed fraud.

Experience exaggerations. Vendors highlight past projects to prove capability. But references can be inflated and roles embellished. When a vendor claims credit for a project, find out what they actually did.

Capacity mismatches. Some vendors promise more than they can deliver. A two-person shop claims it can staff a major project. Check whether capacity matches promises.

Subcontracting surprises. Proposals promise experienced staff—but after winning, the vendor subs out the work. The team that sold the project never shows up.

False certifications. Contracting programs require vendors to certify status—small business, minority-owned, veteran-owned. Fraud happens when businesses claim status they don't qualify for.

Broken proposal promises. Compare what vendors promised to what they delivered. When reality falls far short, either the vendor lied or the agency isn't holding them accountable.

Using Red Flags Effectively

A single red flag doesn't prove wrongdoing. But red flags tell you where to focus. When you spot one, look for others. Problems tend to cluster.

Ask yourself: Is there an innocent explanation? Sometimes there is. Short timelines might reflect genuine urgency. Sole-source contracts might be justified. But when explanations seem weak—or when nobody documented them—keep digging.

Document what you find. Note specific records, dates, names, and amounts. Quote key contract language. Build your own paper trail.

Remember: you're not a prosecutor. You don't have to prove crimes beyond reasonable doubt. Your job is to ask questions, surface information, and bring attention to problems that deserve scrutiny. Sometimes that leads to investigations. Sometimes it leads to reforms. Sometimes it just leads to better decisions next time.

Spotting Conflicts of Interest

When investigating potential conflicts, request:

- Financial disclosure forms filed by relevant officials
- Vendor registration documents showing company ownership
- Scoring committee membership lists
- Recusal records showing when officials removed themselves from decisions
- Ethics opinions requested about potential conflicts

Sometimes connections aren't direct. Look for:

- Subcontractor relationships where the conflict is one level removed
- Consulting arrangements between officials and vendors
- Shared business addresses or registered agents
- Similar patterns across multiple contracts

A connection doesn't automatically mean corruption. Officials in small communities often have legitimate business relationships with local companies. The key: was the relationship properly disclosed and handled according to ethics rules?

Connecting Different Records

The most effective analysis connects different types of records:

- Compare the original RFP with the final contract. Did terms change?
- Cross-reference payments with deliverables. Was work completed before payment?
- Read meeting minutes alongside contract amendments. What justified the changes?
- Check inspection reports against contract specifications. Did the work comply?

Connecting dots often reveals issues no single document would show.

Maria's Journey: Reading the Contract

The complete contract package arrived: main agreement, seven exhibits, three amendments. Over 120 pages. Maria spread them across her dining room table after the kids were asleep.

She started with the main contract's structure. Scope of Work. Payment Terms. Timeline. Performance Standards. She made a simple outline: what Sundagger was supposed to deliver, and when.

The payment schedule stopped her. Sundagger would receive 80% of the total amount upon signing—before any work began.

She texted Joseph: "Is this normal?"

"No. Usually they pay in stages as work gets done. Note that."

Next, the bidding documents. Three companies had submitted proposals. Sundagger scored highest on "Experience" and "Project Approach"—but their bid was $320,000 higher than the lowest bidder. The selection memo said the extra cost was justified by "superior qualifications." No specifics.

Maria pulled the individual scoring sheets. Two evaluators gave Sundagger perfect scores in every category. The third—the city engineer—rated them much lower on "technical approach" and "past performance."

She checked the other three Sundagger contracts she'd requested. Same pattern. Two perfect scores. One skeptic overruled.

The campaign contribution forms arrived the following week. Sundagger's owner had given the maximum allowed to the mayor and to two council members. Both council members had voted yes on the contract.

Maria wrote up what she'd found:

1. 80% payment upfront, before work started
2. Two evaluators consistently overriding the city engineer
3. Campaign contributions from the contractor to officials who approved the deal
4. No real explanation for picking the higher bid

The records didn't prove anything illegal. But they showed a pattern worth asking about.

PART 5

BUILDING YOUR INVESTIGATION

The Strategic Approach

Investigating government spending rarely happens with a single records request. Think of it like building a house—you lay the foundation before adding walls. Each request builds on what you learned from the last one.

Here's how to construct your investigation step by step.

Start with the Rules

Before you can spot rule-breaking, you need to know the rules. Even agencies covered by the Procurement Code often have their own policies that add requirements. Your first requests should establish what's supposed to happen:

- Procurement policies and procedures (often called a "procurement manual")

- Memoranda with additional requirements or guidance
- Internal procedures for contract approval
- Delegation of authority documents showing who can approve what dollar amounts
- Conflict of interest policies and disclosure requirements

These documents create your baseline. They tell you how things should work—so you can measure how they actually work.

They also give you clues about what other documents should exist. If the policy says every purchase over $10,000 requires three quotes, you now know to request those quotes. For example, if the manual says that sole-source contracts require certain documents, you know those documents should exist.

Get the Contracts

With the rules in hand, request the actual contracts you're investigating. Ask for:

- The full executed contract with all exhibits and attachments
- All proposals and bids submitted—not just the winner
- The purchase order or payment authorization
- Contractor qualification or verification documents

Don't just look at price and scope. Pay attention to payment terms, performance metrics, and termination clauses. These show what leverage the government has if things go wrong.

Follow the Money

Contracts tell you what was supposed to happen. Payment records show what actually happened.

Request:

- All invoices submitted by the contractor
- Payment records showing amounts and dates
- Documentation of work completion or milestone achievement
- Budget transfer records if additional funds were allocated

Look for discrepancies. Are payments happening before deliverables are complete? Do invoices match agreed-upon rates? Does the total paid match the contract amount—or exceed it?

Track Changes

Few contracts execute exactly as written. Changes happen, but they should follow proper procedures.

Request:

- All amendments to the original contract
- Change orders that modified scope, timeline, or price
- Communications about justifications for changes
- Approval documentation for each change

Pay special attention to price increases. Some changes are legitimate—you can't predict everything. But patterns of dramatic cost escalation after contract award deserve scrutiny. A contract that doubles in price through change orders may signal poor planning, scope manipulation, or worse.

Check the Oversight

Someone should verify that work meets standards. Request:

- Inspection reports for construction or physical deliverables
- Performance evaluations of the contractor

- Documentation of contract disputes or performance issues
- Records of corrective actions or penalties assessed

The absence of documentation can be as telling as its presence. A multi-million dollar construction project with no inspection reports is a red flag. Either oversight didn't happen, or records are missing.

Look Beyond the Contracting Agency

A thorough investigation often leads to multiple agencies. Relevant documents may exist elsewhere:

- Building permits from local planning departments
- Environmental inspection reports from state regulators
- Audits by the State Auditor or federal oversight agencies
- Licensing records from regulatory boards
- Campaign finance records from the Secretary of State

Don't limit yourself to the agency that signed the contract.

Managing a Growing Investigation

As your investigation expands, organization becomes critical.

Build a timeline. Plot key events and decisions in order. When was the RFP issued? When did bidding close? When was the contract signed? When did payments start? Timelines reveal patterns—rushed approvals, retroactive paperwork, suspicious sequences.

Track the money. Use a spreadsheet to log contracts, amendments, and payments. Include dates, amounts, and document sources. Running totals show whether spending matches authorizations.

Map the relationships. Document connections between people, companies, and projects. Who approved what? Which officials have ties to which vendors? Do the same names keep appearing?

Note the gaps. When policy says a document should exist but you can't find it, record that. Missing records matter.

Submit Follow-Up Requests

If information seems incomplete, ask again. Agencies sometimes fail to search for responsive documents in all departments.

Try different angles:

- Ask a different department
- Use different search terms
- Request records from a different time period
- Ask for communications instead of formal documents

Phrasing your request slightly differently may route it to different staff—producing dramatically different results.

Keep Your Own Records

Document your investigation as carefully as you document the agency's actions:

- Save every request you submit
- Record submission dates and methods
- Keep all responses, even unhelpful ones
- Note who you communicated with
- Screenshot online submissions

If your investigation leads to a formal complaint, lawsuit, or news story, you'll need to show your work.

Maria's Journey: Going Deeper

Maria taped a timeline to her dining room wall. Contract approvals. Payments. Campaign contributions. Seeing the dates together revealed patterns she'd missed before.

Her next round of requests:

1. All emails between the Mayor or Deputy City Manager and Sundagger Ventures, January 2021 to present
2. Minutes from meetings where Sundagger contracts were discussed before formal approval
3. Financial disclosure forms from the two evaluators who gave Sundagger perfect scores
4. Any ethics opinions about conflicts of interest related to these contracts

The city said the email request would take "additional time" due to volume. Maria narrowed it: just the three months before each contract approval. Harder to call that too broad.

The emails arrived two weeks later. Most were routine. But one stood out: the Deputy City Manager advising Sundagger on "positioning your proposal for maximum points"—weeks before the RFP went public.

"Other bidders didn't get that heads-up," Joseph said.

Maria also found that one evaluator—the one who always gave Sundagger perfect scores—had previously worked for a company owned by Sundagger's founder. That relationship didn't appear on his financial disclosure form.

She built a system to track everything:

- Separate folders for each contract
- A spreadsheet logging every request, response, and follow-up
- A contact list noting each player's role and connections
- Page references linking each finding to source documents

After her third round of requests, the city clerk called. Why did she need "all these detailed records"? She was "creating unnecessary work."

"I'm exercising my right under IPRA to inspect records related to how taxpayer money is spent," Maria said. "These requests are specific and focused on public business."

The clerk backed down.

PART 6

DEALING WITH PUSHBACK

When Agencies Resist

Even well-crafted requests sometimes hit roadblocks. Agencies may have legitimate constraints—or they may be trying to avoid scrutiny. Knowing how to respond keeps your investigation on track.

"Your Request Is Too Broad"

This is the most common pushback for contract-related requests.

First, evaluate honestly. Is your request actually too broad? If you asked for "all contracts from the past five years," the agency has a point.

If they're right: Narrow your request to what you really need. Specify departments, date ranges, dollar thresholds, or vendor names.

If they're wrong: Push back in writing. Explain why your request is reasonable. Mention similar requests they've fulfilled. Point out that the records should be easily accessible in their financial system.

Sample response:

> I understand your concern about scope. To clarify, I'm seeking only contracts between your agency and ABC Consulting from January 2022 to present. Your public meeting minutes indicate approximately 3-5 such contracts exist. This narrowed request should not be excessively burdensome.

"No Responsive Records Exist"

Sometimes agencies claim they can't find what you're looking for.

First, check your terminology. Different agencies use different terms for similar documents. A "contract" might be filed as a "professional services agreement" or "memorandum of understanding." Getting the agency's procurement manual helps you use their language.

Then, request related records that would reference what you're seeking. If they claim no contract exists, ask for:

- Payment records to that vendor
- Purchase orders
- Meeting minutes where the expenditure was approved
- Budget documents showing the line item

If these secondary records exist, they prove the primary records should exist too.

Sample response:

> Thank you for your response. I'm surprised no contract with ABC Consulting exists, as your February board meeting minutes reference approving a $250,000 contract with this vendor. Please search again, and if no contract is found, please provide any documents showing how this payment was authorized.

"These Records Are Exempt"

Agencies sometimes claim contracts contain exempt information.

First, demand specifics. Which exemption are they claiming? Which portions of the records are affected? The presence of some exempt information doesn't justify withholding entire documents.

Then, request redacted versions with only the exempt information removed. IPRA requires agencies to separate exempt from non-exempt material and provide everything that isn't exempt.

Sample response:

> I understand some information in these contracts may be exempt. However, IPRA requires you to separate exempt from non-exempt information and provide the non-exempt portions. Please provide redacted copies with only the specifically exempt information removed. Include a written explanation identifying each exemption claimed and the material it covers.

"We Need Payment First"

Agencies can require advance payment for copying costs. But they can only charge what IPRA allows.

Know the limits:

- **Paper copies:** Maximum $1.00 per page for standard sizes (11" x 17" or smaller)
- **Electronic copies:** No per-page fee. The agency can only charge for the storage device (like a thumb drive) and actual transmission costs (postage or shipping)
- **Staff time:** No charge for time spent searching, reviewing, or redacting records
- **Inspection:** Free. You can always view records in person at no cost

That last point matters. You have the right to inspect records without paying anything. You only pay when you want copies.

Cost-saving strategies:

- Request electronic copies instead of paper—often free or nearly free
- Inspect records in person first, then request copies of only the most important pages
- Narrow your request to essential documents
- Ask for a copy of the agency's IPRA fee schedule

IPRA does not have a formal fee waiver provision. Instead, IPRA allows agencies to charge for copies of records (but not inspections) up the amounts listed in the law itself. The agency can charge those fees even if you have a good reason to request the records and even if you are indigent.

But you can still ask for a waiver or reduction of fees. The agency is not obligated to do so, but you might get lucky.

Challenging Excessive Fees

If you receive a high fee estimate, question it. Agencies sometimes overcharge—whether from misunderstanding IPRA or hoping you'll go away.

Sample challenge:

> Your fee estimate of $500 seems excessive under IPRA. The 50-page contract should cost no more than $50 at the maximum rate of $1.00 per page. Please provide a detailed breakdown. Note that IPRA prohibits charging for staff time spent searching or reviewing records.

For electronic records, push back harder:

> You've estimated $200 for electronic copies of these documents. Under IPRA, agencies cannot charge per-page fees for electronic records—only the actual cost of storage media. A thumb drive costs less than $10. Please revise this estimate.

Keeping Records of the Dispute

When agencies push back, document everything:

- Save all correspondence
- Note dates of phone calls and what was said

- Screenshot online portal messages
- Keep copies of your follow-up requests

This documentation becomes evidence if you need to escalate.

When to Consider Legal Help

Many IPRA disputes resolve through persistent follow-up. But sometimes you need an attorney. Consider legal help when:

- The agency has ignored multiple requests
- Delays have stretched months beyond legal deadlines
- The agency claims an exemption that clearly doesn't apply
- You have evidence records exist despite denials
- The agency closed your request without producing all responsive documents
- The records involve significant public interest

The fee-shifting advantage: IPRA requires agencies to pay your attorney fees if you win in court. This encourages lawyers to take legitimate cases even when clients can't pay upfront. Many attorneys will evaluate IPRA cases on contingency—they get paid only if you prevail.

When you consult an attorney, bring:

- Copies of all your requests
- All agency responses
- Evidence of what records should exist
- A timeline of your interactions with the agency
- Notes on why you believe the agency violated IPRA

The stronger your documentation, the easier it is for an attorney to evaluate your case.

Maria's Journey: Pushback

After Maria's discovery about the undisclosed relationship, the city's tone changed.

Her next request—communications between Sundagger and the Planning Department—hit a wall. The clerk called it "excessively burdensome" and claimed it would take "many months."

Maria narrowed the request:

> I'm happy to limit this to communications between the Planning Director and Sundagger Ventures during March–May 2023, when the Main Street project was being evaluated. One employee, three months. Please let me know if this allows you to proceed.

Three days later: "Your modified request has been received."

At the next council meeting, the Deputy City Manager approached her during a break.

"I understand you've been requesting a lot of records about Sundagger. May I ask what your concern is?"

"I'm researching city contracting processes," Maria said. "IPRA gives every citizen the right to inspect public records without explaining why."

"Of course. It's just that processing these requests takes staff time away from serving the public."

"Transparency is a public service too."

A week later, the city sent a fee estimate: $235 for copying costs.

Maria responded:

> Since IPRA allows electronic copies to reduce costs, I'd prefer digital format. If any documents exist only on paper, I'd like to inspect them in person before deciding which ones need copies.

The city provided the records electronically at no cost.

But something was off. The emails stopped cold for two weeks in April, then picked up with references to meetings that had clearly happened during the gap.

Maria followed up:

> I've noticed no emails between April 10–24, despite references to meetings during this period in later messages. Could you verify that all responsive records from this timeframe have been provided?

The clerk called. "We're looking into this. There may have been some miscommunication about which accounts to search."

A week later, more emails arrived. The Planning Director had been using a personal account for city business. One message read: "Let's continue this conversation on my Gmail to keep it out of the city system."

CONNECTING THE DOTS

From Documents to Understanding

Getting records is only half the battle. Now you need to figure out what they mean.

This chapter walks you through a practical process for analyzing government records. The goal: move from a pile of documents to a clear picture of what happened—and whether anything went wrong.

Step 1: Organize Before You Analyze

When records arrive, resist the urge to dive in. Organize first.

Rename files. Agencies often use meaningless names like "Doc001.pdf." Rename files so you can find things later. "2024-03-15_Contract_ABCPaving.pdf" tells you something. "Doc001.pdf" tells you nothing. I like to start each filename with a date in YYYY-MM-DD format. That lets you quickly organize documents chronologically.

Create folders. Group related documents together. Emails from the same person. All contracts in one place. Invoices together. Meeting minutes in their own folder. This makes review manageable. For example, you might create a main folder name for your investigations, with subfolders for different aspects of your investigation.

Build a master list. Open a spreadsheet. List every document you received with a brief description. When you find something important later, you'll be able to locate it again.

This upfront work pays off. Without organization, you'll waste hours hunting for that one email you remember seeing somewhere.

Step 2: Break the Work Into Chunks

A thousand pages feels overwhelming. Fifty pages at a time feels doable.

Use your folder system to create natural chunks. Today: emails from the project manager. Tomorrow: invoices. Next day: meeting minutes.

If you're facing a mountain of documents, AI tools can help. Upload files to ChatGPT or Claude and ask specific questions: "Find all references to payments over $50,000" or "List every mention of subcontractors." This won't replace careful reading, but it can point you to what matters most.

Step 3: Your First Pass

On your first read-through, do three things at once.

Build a timeline. Note key events in chronological order. Putting things in sequence often reveals the story.

Create a simple spreadsheet. For example, I might start with just a few columns:

Date	Document	Page	Notes
6/15/2025	June Minutes.pdf	3	City Council Authorized RPF
6/28/2025	Screenshot	n/a	RFP published on City website
6/28/2025	RFP.pdf	22	Scoring criteria includes experience with telecommunications projects

Adjust columns based on your investigation. If you're tracking payments, include amounts and approvers. If you're following a construction project, include milestones and inspections.

Spot gaps. Watch for references to documents you don't have.

- An email shows an attachment icon—where's the attachment?
- A contract mentions "the authorizing resolution"—did you receive it?
- Meeting minutes reference a "board packet"—what was in it?
- Someone writes "Let me know your feedback on the draft"— where's the draft?

These clues tell you records are missing. Flag them for follow-up requests.

Note red flags. When something looks off, mark it. Apply the warning signs from Part 4. Don't stop to investigate each flag on your first pass. Just note it and keep moving. You'll come back later.

Step 4: Compare Rules to Reality

This is where analysis gets powerful.

Every government spending decision follows rules—procurement codes, grant regulations, agency policies. These rules spell out what should happen: how contracts get approved, who signs off on payments, what disclosures are required.

Your timeline shows what actually happened.

Put them side by side. Look for conflicts.

- The procurement manual says contracts over $25,000 need three competitive bids. Did this contract get three bids?
- Grant guidelines require quarterly progress reports. Were they filed?
- Policy says city council must approve contracts over $100,000. Did the council vote?
- Conflict-of-interest rules require disclosure before voting. Did the official disclose?

To make this comparison, you need the governing rules. You should have requested these early in your investigation. If you didn't, request them now: "The procurement code, procurement manual, and any policy memos governing [the type of spending you're investigating]."

Step 5: Verify Against Outside Sources

Records can lie. People misrepresent facts on paper. Verify what you can.

Check credentials. A contractor claimed to be a licensed electrician? Search the Construction Industries Division website.

Confirm disclosures. Someone said they disclosed campaign contributions? Look up the actual filings with the Secretary of State.

Search for conflicts. A vendor certified no conflicts of interest? Search court records for lawsuits involving the decision-makers.

Cross-check related documents. Compare what different records say about the same thing:

- Does the scope of work in the RFP match the signed contract?
- Does the approved budget match actual payments?
- Do meeting minutes reflect what emails said behind the scenes?
- Does the contractor's proposal match what they delivered?

Discrepancies between documents often reveal problems that no single document would show.

Step 6: Fill the Gaps

When you identify missing documents, act fast.

First question: Should it have been produced already? If an email clearly had an attachment and you didn't receive it, that's a gap in the agency's response. Follow up in writing. If they still don't produce it, you may have grounds for enforcement.

Second question: Was it outside your earlier request's scope? If so, file a new request. Don't wait until you've finished your entire review. Agencies take weeks to respond. Get follow-up requests moving now.

You can have multiple requests pending at once. Submitting them one at a time, waiting for each response before sending the next, is a recipe for an investigation that drags on for months.

Step 7: Know When You Have Enough

When are you done? This judgment gets easier with experience.

Look for corroboration. Can you support critical facts from multiple sources? If three different documents point to the same conclusion, you're on solid ground. If you're relying on a single email to prove your entire case, keep digging.

Check your timeline. Is it complete? Do you understand the sequence of events—who did what and when? Have you filled the gaps you identified?

Test your conclusions. For each problem you've identified, ask: What's the innocent explanation? Have you ruled it out? If someone challenged your findings, could you defend them with evidence?

The Mistake That Trips Up Beginners

The most common error: rushing to judgment.

Someone finds one damning email and concludes they've cracked the case. But that email might look different with context. Maybe another email explains the situation. Maybe the rules allowed an exception. Maybe the person who wrote it was misinformed.

Take your time. Build evidence carefully. Make sure each critical fact has support before you draw conclusions.

This isn't just about fairness—it's about effectiveness. If you go public with accusations based on a single document, and it turns out you missed context, you lose credibility. Your legitimate concerns get dismissed.

Patient, thorough analysis produces results you can stand behind.

When Records Are Missing or Destroyed

Sometimes agencies respond with the words no requester wants to hear: "These records no longer exist."

That answer might be true. Government offices don't keep everything forever. Retention schedules require agencies to destroy certain records after set periods. Emails get purged. Old files get shredded.

But "we don't have it" isn't always the end of the story. Here's how to push back—and how to work around the gap.

You Can't Sue Over Destroyed Records

First, the hard truth. IPRA governs access to records. It doesn't govern retention. If an agency destroyed records it should have kept, that may violate the Public Records Act or other retention rules. But there's no private right of action—meaning you can't sue them for it.

That doesn't mean violations go unaddressed. Consider filing complaints with:

- **State Records Center and Archives:** They oversee records retention compliance for state and local agencies. A complaint may trigger an investigation or audit.
- **State Ethics Commission:** If the destruction seems connected to misconduct—like officials covering their tracks—ethical violations may be implicated.

These complaints won't get you the missing records. But they create accountability and may prevent future "disappearances."

The Records May Exist Somewhere Else

Just because one agency doesn't have a document doesn't mean it's gone. Ask yourself: who else might have a copy?

- **State Records Center and Archives:** Agencies transfer older records here. What the agency purged from active files may sit in archival storage.
- **Other agencies involved in the same matter:** A contract between the city and a vendor exists in the city's files—but also in the vendor's. Correspondence between two departments exists in both. If Agency A destroyed its copy, Agency B might still have theirs.
- **Oversight bodies:** Auditors, inspectors general, and legislative committees often receive copies of key documents. Their files may preserve what the original agency lost.

Submit new requests to these alternative sources. You may recover exactly what you need.

Reconstruct What's Missing

Even if the original document is gone, other records may tell you what it said.

- Meeting minutes might summarize a report that no longer exists.
- Emails might reference or quote from a destroyed memo.
- Later documents might incorporate earlier findings.
- Responses to the original document reveal what it contained.

Think creatively. Request records that would have referenced, responded to, or relied on the missing document. Piece together the substance from what survives.

Challenge Whether the Search Was Adequate

"We don't have it" sometimes means "we didn't look hard enough."

Agencies often search only the obvious places. An email search might turn up nothing because the server purges messages after ninety days. But what about:

- **Desktop computers:** Employees save drafts and final versions locally. Were individual workstations searched?
- **Shared drives:** Departments maintain network folders outside the email system.
- **Backup systems:** Even "deleted" records may exist on backup tapes or disaster recovery systems.
- **Personal devices:** If employees used personal phones or email for government business—which they shouldn't, but sometimes do—records may exist there.

Push back in writing: "Please confirm whether the search included desktop computers, shared network drives, and backup systems. If not, please expand the search to include these locations."

Request the Retention Policies

Ask for the agency's records retention schedule and any policies governing the type of document you're seeking. Then compare:

- How long should this record have been kept?
- When was it supposedly destroyed?
- Does the timeline match the policy?

If an agency claims it destroys emails after one year but you're asking about correspondence from six months ago, something doesn't add up. Retention policies give you a baseline to test the agency's story.

Look for Suspicious Patterns

Not all missing records are equal. Context matters.

Normal pattern: An agency has no records from more than five years ago. Their retention schedule requires destruction after five years. The gap is consistent and explainable.

Suspicious pattern: An agency has comprehensive files going back a decade—except for documents directly relevant to your investigation. That gap suggests either current withholding disguised as "destruction" or past tampering.

When gaps appear selective, document the pattern. Note what exists on either side of the hole. A timeline showing "we have everything except this" is powerful evidence that something is wrong.

Document Everything

Whether the records are truly gone or suspiciously missing, keep detailed notes:

- Exactly what the agency claimed
- When they claimed it
- What retention policies say
- What alternative sources you tried
- What patterns you observed

If you later pursue complaints, litigation, or public pressure, this documentation builds your case. Even if the original records are gone, the story of their disappearance can be just as revealing.

Maria's Journey: Connecting the Dots

Two months of requests had produced hundreds of pages. Maria organized her analysis around specific questions, one issue at a time.

First, the payment structure. She built a table comparing Sundagger's contracts with three other vendors:

Vendor	Initial Payment
Sundagger (4 contracts)	30–80% upfront
Other vendors (3 contracts)	10–15% upfront

Next, the bid evaluations. She created a spreadsheet: all bidders, their proposed costs, each evaluator's scores by category. The same two evaluators gave Sundagger near-perfect scores on all four contracts, overriding lower scores from technical staff. In three cases, Sundagger wasn't the lowest bidder but won anyway.

Then the timeline:

- **January 2021:** Campaign contributions from Sundagger's owner to the Mayor and two council members
- **March 2021:** Deputy City Manager emails "guidance" to Sundagger before the RFP goes public
- **April 2021:** RFP issued
- **May 2021:** Evaluation committee formed—includes two members with ties to Sundagger
- **June 2021:** Contract awarded despite being $320,000 higher than lowest bid
- **July 2021:** 80% payment processed

This pattern repeated for the next three contracts.

The emails filled in the gaps:

- The Planning Director using personal email to "keep it out of the city system"
- The Deputy City Manager referencing "our agreement" with Sundagger before bidding opened
- An evaluator asking Sundagger's owner how to "address the engineer's concerns"

Maria's final summary ran 12 pages:

1. Payment structure irregularities
2. Bid evaluation patterns
3. Undisclosed relationships
4. Procedural violations
5. Timeline of key events

Each finding cited specific documents. Where the city had refused to provide records, she noted the gap.

PART 8

TAKING ACTION

From Information to Impact

Finding problems through IPRA is only half the battle. The real goal is change—better oversight, stronger accountability, smarter spending.

This chapter covers how to make your findings matter.

Prepare a Clear Summary

Before contacting anyone, organize your findings into a concise, factual document.

Keep it brief. One to three pages works for most situations. Save detailed documentation as backup.

Stick to facts. Focus on what the records show. Avoid speculation. Use specific numbers and dates.

Include key evidence. Attach copies of the most important documents. Screenshots of damning emails or contract provisions can be powerful.

Stay neutral. This is critical. Words like "corruption," "fraud," or "criminal" are less effective than a clear presentation of facts. Let the evidence speak. Your goal is to persuade people who may be skeptical. Accusations make them defensive. Facts make them pay attention.

Add visuals when helpful. Timelines showing the sequence of events. Charts comparing contract amounts to market rates. Tables listing payments that exceeded approved budgets. Visual presentation makes complex information accessible.

Where to Take Your Findings

Different problems call for different channels. Consider these options based on what you've uncovered:

For procurement and policy violations:

- The agency's department head or administrator
- The governing body (city council, county commission, school board)
- The agency's inspector general or internal auditor, if one exists

For ethics violations:

- New Mexico State Ethics Commission
- Relevant professional licensing boards

For financial misconduct or fraud:

- New Mexico Department of Justice
- State Auditor's Office
- New Mexico State Police or local law enforcement

For election-related issues:

- New Mexico Secretary of State

For systemic problems requiring public pressure:

- Elected officials who might champion reforms
- Civic organizations focused on government accountability
- Media—traditional newspapers and TV, but also investigative podcasts, blogs, and local news websites

For exploring legal options:

- Private attorneys who handle government accountability cases

You may pursue multiple channels at once. A complaint to the State Auditor doesn't prevent you from also presenting at a public meeting or talking to a reporter.

Using Public Comment Periods

Most governing bodies—city councils, county commissions, school boards—allow public comment at their meetings. This creates a powerful opportunity to put your findings on the official record.

Prepare written remarks. Most bodies limit comments to two or three minutes. Write out what you'll say and time yourself.

Bring copies. Give one to each board member and one for the official record. Your written statement becomes part of the minutes.

Focus on facts and impact. Explain what you found and why it matters to the community. Don't ramble or editorialize.

Make a specific ask. Request an audit. Ask for a policy change. Demand an explanation. Give them something concrete to respond to.

Follow up in writing. After the meeting, send a letter summarizing your concerns and your request. Create a paper trail showing the body was informed.

Your public comments become part of the official record. If officials later claim they didn't know about the problem, you have proof they did.

The Fraud Against Taxpayers Act

New Mexico's Fraud Against Taxpayers Act (FATA) provides another avenue when you've uncovered serious financial misconduct.

What FATA allows: Private citizens can file lawsuits on behalf of the state against individuals or companies that defraud the government. This includes knowingly submitting false claims for payment, using fake records to get paid, or conspiring to cheat the government.

The potential recovery: Successful lawsuits can recover three times the government's damages plus penalties. The person who brings the case—called a "relator"—can receive 15 to 30 percent of the recovery.

How it differs from IPRA: FATA addresses fraud, not transparency. The burden of proof is much higher. You'll need an attorney experienced in these cases. The lawsuit initially stays sealed while the government investigates.

When FATA makes sense:

- You've found evidence of deliberate fraud—not just mistakes or policy violations

- The financial harm is substantial
- You have strong documentary evidence (IPRA records work well here)
- Other remedies haven't produced results

FATA cases are complex. But they can be powerful tools for recovering public money and holding fraudsters accountable.

Handling Pushback

When you bring problems to light, expect resistance. Here's how to respond:

"This is how it's always been done." Point to better practices in other jurisdictions. Just because something is traditional doesn't make it legal or wise.

"You don't understand the complexity." Acknowledge that government procurement is complicated. Then refocus on the specific problem you've documented. Complexity isn't an excuse for violating the rules.

"We're already addressing this internally." Ask for documentation. What specific steps are being taken? What's the timeline? Request records showing the corrective action.

"This is just a political attack." Emphasize that your concerns are based on documented facts from public records. You're not attacking anyone—you're asking questions the public deserves answered.

Stay professional. Focus on issues, not personalities. Your credibility is your most valuable asset. Once you're seen as a crank or a partisan, your legitimate concerns get dismissed.

The Ripple Effect

Sometimes the biggest impact isn't fixing one problem. It's creating a culture where problems don't happen in the first place.

When officials know their decisions will face scrutiny, they're more likely to follow proper procedures. When procurement staff know someone might request the bid documents, they're more careful about the process. When contractors know their invoices could be examined, they're less likely to overbill.

This may be the most important part of your work: reminding officials that people are watching and preventing problems before they happen.

You may never know how many corners didn't get cut because someone knew you were watching. But that invisible impact is real. It's democracy working the way it should.

Maria's Journey: Going Public

Maria had a fact-based case. Now she needed to use it.

She planned three moves: present to the council, share with local media, connect with the state auditor.

The council gave her three minutes. She focused on three findings:

1. The undisclosed relationship between an evaluator and Sundagger
2. The Planning Director's use of personal email to avoid public records
3. The pattern of large upfront payments

She prepared a one-page handout with a link to the full documents.

At the podium, she kept it direct: "I'm sharing findings about city contracts with Sundagger Ventures, based entirely on public records obtained through IPRA."

Council members looked up from their phones. The city manager stopped typing.

"These aren't accusations. They're documented facts about how public money is being spent. I've prepared copies for each of you, with references to the source records."

When her time expired, the mayor tried to move on. Councilor Herrera stopped him.

"I'd like to request a formal investigation. These are serious issues backed by public records."

Two other council members agreed. The mayor added it to the next agenda.

Outside, a reporter approached. "Do you really have documents backing all that up?"

Maria handed him a USB drive. "Every word."

That Sunday, the newspaper ran a front-page story: "Records Reveal Questionable Contract Patterns." Two other citizens filed their own IPRA requests, building on her work.

Maria sent her findings to the state auditor. Three weeks later, they opened a preliminary inquiry.

By the next council meeting, the Planning Director was on administrative leave. All Sundagger contracts were under review. The mayor announced a task force on procurement reform.

A month later, the city adopted new policies: stricter disclosure requirements, limits on upfront payments, mandatory documentation of evaluation decisions.

At the next neighborhood meeting, people asked Maria for help with their own requests.

"You don't need to be a lawyer," she told them. "Be specific. Be persistent. Follow up."

PART 9

WORKING WITH A LAWYER

Making the Most of Your Consultation

When an agency won't comply with your request, a lawyer can help. But legal consultations cost money—yours or the attorney's, depending on the fee arrangement. Come prepared to make every minute count.

What to Bring

Gather these documents before your meeting:

Your original request:

- The exact request you submitted, with the date
- Proof you sent it (email receipt, certified mail slip, portal screenshot)
- Any clarifications you provided later

Agency responses:

- The acknowledgment letter (the "three-day letter")
- Status updates, emails, or letters about your request
- The denial letter, if you received one
- Any records the agency provided, even if incomplete

Your timeline:

- A chronological list of every interaction
- Notes from phone calls (with names and dates)
- Copies of your follow-up communications

Evidence the records exist:

- Public references to the records (meeting minutes, news articles, budget documents)
- Similar records you've received before
- Anything proving the agency has what you requested

How to Organize Your Packet

Create a simple packet with four sections.

Section 1: One-Page Summary

Start with a clear overview:

- Who you requested records from
- What you requested (briefly)
- When you submitted the request
- What happened (or didn't)
- Why you believe the agency violated IPRA

Keep this to one page. The lawyer needs to grasp your situation quickly.

Section 2: Timeline

Create a chronological list of events:

June 1, 2024: Submitted request for contract documents via email

June 5, 2024: Received acknowledgment letter; agency said records would be ready by June 16

June 16, 2024: Deadline passed; no records received

June 17, 2024: Sent follow-up email

June 24, 2024: Agency claimed request was "too broad"

June 25, 2024: Sent narrowed request with specific contract numbers

July 15, 2024: Still no response

Dates matter in IPRA cases. A clear timeline shows exactly where the agency fell short.

Section 3: Specific Violations

Identify which IPRA requirements you believe were violated:

- Missed the 15-day deadline
- Failed to provide a written explanation of denial
- Claimed an exemption that doesn't apply
- Produced some records but not all, without explanation
- Charged fees IPRA doesn't allow

Be specific. "They violated IPRA" isn't helpful. "They missed the 15-day deadline by 45 days and never explained why" is.

Section 4: Supporting Documents

Include copies of key documents. Label them clearly. Organize them in the same order as your timeline.

Questions the Lawyer Will Ask

Think through these before your meeting:

About your request:

- What's your connection to this issue?
- Why do you need these records? (IPRA doesn't require a reason, but context helps the lawyer understand your case.)
- Have you requested similar records before?
- Did you try narrowing your request when asked?

About the agency's response:

- Did they cite a specific IPRA exemption?
- Did they explain which records they're withholding and why?
- Have they provided anything at all?
- Have they shown any willingness to work with you?

About what you want:

- What's your ideal outcome—getting the records, changing agency practices, or both?
- Is timing critical? Do you need records for an upcoming meeting or deadline?
- Would you accept a settlement that provides some but not all records?
- Are you willing to go to court if necessary?

Assessing Your Case Strength

Before your meeting, honestly evaluate where you stand.

Stronger cases typically involve:

- Clear violations of specific IPRA requirements
- A well-documented timeline with copies of all communications
- Narrowly tailored requests for specific records
- Records obviously covered by IPRA
- Clear public interest in the information
- A pattern of non-compliance by this agency

Weaker cases may involve:

- Broad or vague requests
- Missing documentation of what you sent and when
- Records that might legitimately fall under an exemption
- Limited public interest
- Genuinely massive requests where some delay is reasonable

An honest self-assessment helps you and the lawyer decide whether to proceed—and how.

Understanding Legal Costs

Legal help costs money, but IPRA cases have options other types of cases don't.

The fee-shifting advantage: If you win an IPRA case in court, the agency pays your attorney fees. This is powerful. It means lawyers may take strong cases on contingency—they get paid only if you prevail. When you consult an attorney, emphasize the strength of your case if you're hoping for a contingency arrangement.

Other ways to manage costs:

- **Free consultations.** Many attorneys offer a free initial meeting to evaluate your case.
- **Limited-scope help.** You might hire a lawyer just to write a demand letter, not to handle the whole case.
- **Flat fees.** Some attorneys charge a set amount for specific tasks, like drafting a complaint.
- **Shared costs.** If others want the same records, consider pooling resources.
- **Pro bono help.** Organizations focused on government transparency sometimes support cases with clear public interest.

What to Expect in Your Consultation

A productive first meeting typically covers:

- **Case assessment.** The lawyer evaluates whether IPRA was violated and how clearly.
- **Strategy options.** These range from a demand letter to formal litigation.
- **Timeline.** How long enforcement might take if you go to court.
- **Costs.** Fee arrangements, potential recovery, and who pays if you win.
- **Next steps.** What happens immediately after the consultation.

Preparation Checklist

Before your meeting, confirm you've done the following:

- Compiled all communications with the agency
- Created a clear timeline of events

- Organized documents chronologically
- Written a one-page summary
- Made copies of everything for the attorney
- Listed specific IPRA provisions you believe were violated
- Identified your ideal outcome
- Considered what compromise you'd accept
- Prepared questions about the process
- Thought about your budget for legal help

Walking in prepared signals that you're serious. It helps the lawyer help you.

CONCLUSION
THE POWER OF IPRA IN YOUR HANDS

Through these pages, we've seen how IPRA transforms abstract notions of "government transparency" into practical reality. What began as Maria's simple question about a development in her neighborhood grew into something more meaningful—a citizen effectively holding her government accountable.

This is the real promise of IPRA. Not just access to documents, but the ability to see patterns, ask better questions, and create positive change in your community.

Everyday Tools for Extraordinary Impact

The tools Maria used are available to every New Mexican:

- The legal right to inspect public records
- A straightforward process for making requests
- Clear timelines for agency responses
- Enforcement mechanisms when agencies resist

But as we've seen, having these tools isn't enough. It's about using them strategically:

- Starting with focused, specific requests

- Building your knowledge step by step
- Connecting documents to see the bigger picture
- Taking meaningful action with what you find

Beyond Documents to Accountability

The most powerful aspect of IPRA isn't just that you can get documents—it's that officials know you can get documents. When government knows its actions will be scrutinized, it behaves differently from the outset.

This preventive effect may be the most important outcome of all. Problems that never happen because of expected transparency don't make headlines, but they save communities from waste, mismanagement, and corruption.

Becoming Your Community's Maria

What if every neighborhood had someone like Maria? Someone willing to ask questions, request documents, and piece together how public decisions are really made?

The truth is, your community needs you to be that person. You don't need specialized training or credentials—just persistence, organization, and the confidence to exercise your rights.

You might start small, with a single request about an issue that matters to you. Over time, as you build experience and confidence, your impact will grow. What begins as curiosity can evolve into meaningful oversight.

The Journey Continues

This book represents a starting point, not an endpoint. Each request you make will teach you something new about how your government works. Each document you analyze will sharpen your understanding of where problems exist and how they might be solved.

There will be frustrations along the way. Not every request will yield what you hope. Some officials will resist transparency. The process may sometimes feel slow and bureaucratic.

But remember what Maria discovered: persistence pays off. The records you need exist. The patterns are there to be found. And when ordinary citizens take the time to look closely at how their government operates, positive change becomes possible.

That's the true promise of IPRA—not just transparency on paper, but accountability in practice.

So pick an issue that matters to you. Craft your first request. Start your own journey toward becoming your community's guardian of good government.

The records are waiting. The power is in your hands.

WHY I WROTE THIS BOOK

I've fought IPRA battles from both sides.

As General Counsel at the New Mexico Attorney General's Office, I saw how state agencies handle records requests—the real challenges and the excuses.

Since opening my own firm in 2018, I've represented people trying to get records out of government. Community activists researching development deals. Prisoners hunting for evidence in their cases. Public employees seeking answers about their own agencies. Citizens demanding accountability from local officials.

Some of my biggest wins came from suing agencies that stonewalled.

The New Mexico Parole Board ignored request after request from my firm for over a year. We sued. The judge ruled in our favor, and the daily penalties added up to hundreds of thousands of dollars. The Board changed how it handles requests after that—not just for my clients, but for everyone.

The Corrections Department went through a similar transformation. After facing legal consequences, they hired a new records custodian and adopted modern tracking software. Before that, they tracked everything on spreadsheets.

Here's what I've learned: when agencies drag their feet on records, they cut people out of decisions that affect their lives. I've represented residents fighting annexation. Community members trying to protect historic buildings. People who needed documents *before* the next council vote—not six months later.

One government official accused me of "abuse of the statute" and said I'd turned IPRA into a "cottage industry." I consider that one of the best reviews my firm has ever received. When records custodians get uncomfortable, I know I'm doing my job.

By the way, when that official retired, the agency offered us a settlement to avoid trial.

GETTING HELP
HOW TO CONTACT 505 LEGAL

When you've hit a wall with a records request, we can help. Here's how to reach us effectively.

What We Need From You

The more organized your materials, the faster we can help. Here's what to send:

Your records request. Send us the exact language you submitted. Include the date you sent it and how you sent it (email, mail, hand delivery).

The agency's responses. Every letter, email, or acknowledgment you received. Include dates.

Your follow-up messages. Copies of every email or letter you sent asking for updates or pushing back on a denial.

The records you did receive. If they gave you partial documents, send those too. Redactions tell a story.

A timeline. Write down what happened and when. Keep it simple:

- June 1: Submitted request to city clerk
- June 4: Received acknowledgment letter

- June 15: No response, sent follow-up email
- July 10: Received partial records with heavy redactions

Fee estimates or invoices. If they're charging money, send the paperwork.

How to Organize Your Materials

- **Make copies of everything.** Never send us your only copy.
- **Put documents in date order.** Oldest first.
- **Don't use staples.** Paper clips or binder clips work better for scanning.
- **Write a short summary.** One page explaining what you asked for, what happened, and what you need help with.

How to Reach Us

The best way to get in touch is through the web at www.505legal.com. You can call us at (505) 421-3329.

If you want to mail us hard copies, use this address:

505 Legal, PC
PO Box 90336
Albuquerque, NM 87199

What to Expect

We review your materials. We'll look at what you sent and figure out whether you have a case worth pursuing.

We may ask for more. Sometimes we need additional documents or details before we can evaluate your situation.

We'll be straight with you. If we can help, we'll tell you how. If we can't, we'll tell you why.

If we take your case, we'll explain next steps. That might mean a demand letter to the agency. Or it might mean filing a lawsuit to enforce your rights.

A Word About Fees

IPRA has teeth. If you win in court, the agency has to pay your attorney's fees. That's the law. See NMSA 1978, § 14-2-12(D).

This means we can sometimes take IPRA cases on contingency—you don't pay unless we win. But every case is different. We'll explain the fee arrangement before any work begins.

If We Can't Take Your Case

We get more inquiries than we can handle. If we turn down your case, it doesn't mean you're wrong. It might just mean we don't have the capacity, or it's not the right fit for our practice.

If that happens:

- Ask us why. We'll try to explain.
- Get a second opinion. Other attorneys handle IPRA cases.
- Keep your records. You may find another path forward.

APPENDIX I
IPRA – FULL TEXT OF THE LAW (2025)

ARTICLE 2

Inspection of Public Records

14-2-1. Right to inspect public records; exceptions.

Every person has a right to inspect public records of this state except:

A. records pertaining to physical or mental examinations and medical treatment of persons confined to an institution;

B. letters of reference concerning employment, licensing or permits;

C. letters or memoranda that are matters of opinion in personnel files or students' cumulative files;

D. portions of law enforcement records as provided in Section 14-2-1.2 NMSA 1978;

E. as provided by the Confidential Materials Act [14-3A-1, 14-3A-2 NMSA 1978];

F. trade secrets;

G. attorney-client privileged information;

H. long-range or strategic business plans of public hospitals discussed in a properly closed meeting;

I. tactical response plans or procedures prepared for or by the state or a political subdivision of the state, the publication of which could reveal specific vulnerabilities, risk assessments or tactical emergency security procedures that could be used to facilitate the planning or execution of a terrorist attack;

J. information concerning information technology systems, the publication of which would reveal specific vulnerabilities that compromise or allow unlawful access to such systems; provided that this subsection shall not be used to restrict requests for:

(1) records stored or transmitted using information technology systems;

(2) internal and external audits of information technology systems, except for those portions that would reveal ongoing vulnerabilities that compromise or allow unlawful access to such systems; or

(3) information to authenticate or validate records received pursuant to a request fulfilled pursuant to the Inspection of Public Records Act;

K. submissions in response to a competitive grant, land lease or scholarship and related scoring materials and evaluation reports until finalists are publicly named or the award is announced;

L. records containing personal identifying information or sensitive information related to the practice of a medical provider employed by a public body who performs medical services related to abortion;

M. case records, third party records, court records and any information gathered in the course of investigations and system monitoring duties by the office of child advocate, pursuant to the provisions of the Office of Child Advocate Act [32A-30-1 to 32A-30-15 NMSA 1978]; and

N. as otherwise provided by law.

14-2-1.1. Personal identifier information.

Protected personal identifier information contained in public records may be redacted by a public body before inspection or copying of a record. The presence of protected personal identifier information on a record does not exempt the record from inspection. Unredacted records that contain protected personal identifier information shall not be made available on publicly accessible websites operated by or managed on behalf of a public body.

14-2-1.2. Law enforcement records.

A. Law enforcement records are public records, except as provided by law and this subsection, and provided that the presence of nonpublic information may be redacted from a written record or digitally obscured in a visual or audio record, including:

(1) before charges are filed, names, addresses, contact information or protected personal identifier information of individuals who are victims of or non-law-enforcement witnesses to an alleged crime of:

(a) assault with intent to commit a violent felony pursuant to Section 30-3-3 NMSA 1978 when the violent felony is criminal sexual penetration;

(b) assault against a household member with intent to commit a violent felony pursuant to Section 30-3-14 NMSA 1978 when the violent felony is criminal sexual penetration;

(c) stalking pursuant to Section 30-3A-3 NMSA 1978;

(d) aggravated stalking pursuant to Section 30-3A-3.1 NMSA 1978;

(e) criminal sexual penetration pursuant to Section 30-9-11 NMSA 1978;

(f) criminal sexual contact pursuant to Section 30-9-12 NMSA 1978; or

(g) sexual exploitation of children pursuant to Section 30-6A-3 NMSA 1978;

(2) before charges are filed, names, addresses, contact information or protected personal identifier information of individuals who are accused but not charged with a crime;

(3) visual depiction of a dead body, unless a law enforcement officer, acting in that capacity, caused or is reasonably alleged or suspected to have caused the death;

(4) visual depiction of great bodily harm, as defined in Section 30-1-12 NMSA 1978, or acts of severe violence resulting in great bodily harm, unless a law enforcement officer, acting in that capacity, caused or is reasonably alleged or suspected to have caused the great bodily harm or act of severe violence;

(5) visual depiction of an individual's intimate body parts, including the genitals, pubic area, anus or postpubescent female

nipple, whether nude or visible through less than opaque clothing;

(6) visual or audio depiction of the notification to a member of the public of a family member's death;

(7) confidential sources, methods or information; or

(8) records pertaining to physical or mental examination and medical treatment of persons unless the information could be relevant to a criminal investigation or an investigation of misfeasance, malfeasance or other suspected violation of law conducted by a person elected to or employed by a public body.

B. A request for release of video or audio shall specify at least one of the following:

(1) the computer-aided dispatch record number;

(2) the police report number;

(3) the date or date range with reasonable specificity and at least one of the following:

(a) the name of a law enforcement officer or first responder;

(b) the approximate time; or

(c) the approximate location; or

(4) other criteria established and published by a law enforcement agency to facilitate access to videos.

C. Except for confidential sources, methods or information, a request to view video or hear audio on-site of a public body is not subject to the restrictions in Subsections A and B of this section. Any recording or copying of video or audio from such viewing or listening is subject to the restrictions in this section.

D. As used in this section, "law enforcement records" includes evidence in any form received or compiled in connection with a criminal investigation or prosecution by a law enforcement or prosecuting agency, including inactive matters or closed investigations to the extent that they contain the information listed in this subsection; provided that the presence of such information on a law enforcement record does not exempt the record from inspection.

14-2-2. Repealed.

14-2-2.1. Copies of public records furnished.

When a copy of any public record is required by the veterans' administration to be used in determining the eligibility of any person to participate in benefits made available by the veterans' administration, the official custodian of such public record shall, without charge, provide the applicant for such benefits, or any person acting on his behalf, or the authorized representative of the veterans' administration, with a certified copy of such record.

14-2-3. Repealed

14-2-4. Short title.

Chapter 14, Article 2 NMSA 1978 may be cited as the "Inspection of Public Records Act".

14-2-5. Purpose of act; declaration of public policy.

Recognizing that a representative government is dependent upon an informed electorate, the intent of the legislature in enacting the

Inspection of Public Records Act [Chapter 14, Article 2 NMSA 1978] is to ensure, and it is declared to be the public policy of this state, that all persons are entitled to the greatest possible information regarding the affairs of government and the official acts of public officers and employees. It is the further intent of the legislature, and it is declared to be the public policy of this state, that to provide persons with such information is an essential function of a representative government and an integral part of the routine duties of public officers and employees.

14-2-6. Definitions.

As used in the Inspection of Public Records Act:

A. "custodian" means any person responsible for the maintenance, care or keeping of a public body's public records, regardless of whether the records are in that person's actual physical custody and control;

B. "file format" means the internal structure of an electronic file that defines the way it is stored and used;

C. "information technology systems" means computer hardware, storage media, networking equipment, physical devices, infrastructure, processes and code, firmware, software and ancillary products and services, including:

(1) systems design and analysis;

(2) development or modification of hardware or solutions used to create, process, store, secure or exchange electronic data;

(3) information storage and retrieval systems;

(4) voice, radio, video and data communication systems;

(5) network, hosting and cloud-based systems;

(6) simulation and testing;

(7) interactions between a user and an information system; and

(8) user and system credentials;

D. "inspect" means to review all public records that are not excluded in Section 14-2-1 NMSA 1978;

E. "person" means any individual, corporation, partnership, firm, association or entity;

F. "protected personal identifier information" means:

(1) all but the last four digits of a:

(a) taxpayer identification number;

(b) financial account number;

(c) credit or debit card number; or

(d) driver's license number;

(2) all but the year of a person's date of birth;

(3) a social security number; and

(4) with regard to a nonelected employee of a public body in the context of the person's employment, the employee's nonbusiness home street address, but not the city, state or zip code;

G. "public body" means the executive, legislative and judicial branches of state and local governments and all advisory boards, commissions, committees, agencies or entities created by the constitution or any branch of government that receives any public funding, including political subdivisions, special taxing districts, school districts and institutions of higher education;

H. "public records" means all documents, papers, letters, books, maps, tapes, photographs, recordings and other materials, regardless of physical form or characteristics, that are used, created, received, maintained or held by or on behalf of any public body and relate to public business, whether or not the records are required by law to be created or maintained; and

I. "trade secret" means trade secret as defined in Subsection D of Section 57-3A-2 NMSA 1978.

14-2-7. Designation of custodian; duties.

Each public body shall designate at least one custodian of public records who shall:

A. receive requests, including electronic mail or facsimile, to inspect public records;

B. respond to requests in the same medium, electronic or paper, in which the request was made in addition to any other medium that the custodian deems appropriate;

C. provide proper and reasonable opportunities to inspect public records;

D. provide reasonable facilities to make or furnish copies of the public records during usual business hours; and

E. post in a conspicuous location at the administrative office and on the publicly accessible web site, if any, of each public body a notice describing:

(1) the right of a person to inspect a public body's records;

(2) procedures for requesting inspection of public records, including the contact information for the custodian of public records;

(3) procedures for requesting copies of public records;

(4) reasonable fees for copying public records; and

(5) the responsibility of a public body to make available public records for inspection.

14-2-8. Procedure for requesting records.

A. Any person wishing to inspect public records may submit an oral or written request to the custodian. However, the procedures set forth in this section shall be in response to a written request. The failure to respond to an oral request shall not subject the custodian to any penalty.

B. Nothing in the Inspection of Public Records Act shall be construed to require a public body to create a public record.

C. A written request shall provide the name, address and telephone number of the person seeking access to the records and shall identify the records sought with reasonable particularity. No person requesting records shall be required to state the reason for inspecting the records.

D. A custodian receiving a written request shall permit the inspection immediately or as soon as is practicable under the circumstances, but not later than fifteen days after receiving a written request. If the inspection is not permitted within three business days, the custodian shall explain in writing when the records will be available for inspection or when the public body will respond to the request. The three-day period shall not begin until the written request is delivered to the office of the custodian.

E. In the event that a written request is not made to the custodian having possession of or responsibility for the public records requested, the person receiving the request shall promptly forward the request to the custodian of the requested public records, if known, and notify the requester. The notification to the requester shall state the reason for the absence of the records from that person's custody or control, the records' location and the name and address of the custodian.

F. For the purposes of this section, "written request" includes an electronic communication, including email or facsimile; provided that the request complies with the requirements of Subsection C of this section.

14-2-9. Procedure for inspection.

A. Requested public records containing information that is exempt and nonexempt from disclosure shall be separated by the custodian prior to inspection, and the nonexempt information shall be made available for inspection. If necessary to preserve the integrity of computer data or the confidentiality of exempt information contained in a database, a partial printout of data containing public records or information may be furnished in lieu of an entire database. Exempt information in an electronic document shall be removed along with the corresponding metadata prior to disclosure by utilizing methods or redaction tools that prevent the recovery of exempt information from a redacted electronic document.

B. A custodian shall provide a copy of a public record in electronic format if the public record is available in electronic format and an electronic copy is specifically requested. However, a custodian is only required to provide the electronic record in the file format in which it exists at the time of the request.

C. A custodian:

    (1) may charge reasonable fees for copying the public records, unless a different fee is otherwise prescribed by law;

    (2) shall not charge fees in excess of one dollar ($1.00) per printed page for documents eleven inches by seventeen inches in size or smaller;

    (3) may charge the actual costs associated with downloading copies of public records to a computer disk or storage device, including the actual cost of the computer disk or storage device;

    (4) may charge the actual costs associated with transmitting copies of public records by mail, electronic mail or facsimile;

    (5) may require advance payment of the fees before making copies of public records;

    (6) shall not charge a fee for the cost of determining whether any public record is subject to disclosure; and

    (7) shall provide a receipt, upon request.

D. Nothing in this section regarding the provision of public data in electronic format shall limit the ability of the custodian to engage in the sale of data as authorized by Sections 14-3-15.1 and 14-3-18 NMSA 1978, including imposing reasonable restrictions on the use of the database and the payment of a royalty or other consideration.

14-2-10. Procedure for excessively burdensome or broad requests.

If a custodian determines that a written request is excessively burdensome or broad, an additional reasonable period of time shall be allowed to comply with the request. The custodian shall provide

Kenneth H. Stalter

written notification to the requester within fifteen days of receipt of the request that additional time will be needed to respond to the written request. The requester may deem the request denied and may pursue the remedies available pursuant to the Inspection of Public Records Act if the custodian does not permit the records to be inspected in a reasonable period of time.

14-2-11. Procedure for denied requests.

A. Unless a written request has been determined to be excessively burdensome or broad, a written request for inspection of public records that has not been permitted within fifteen days of receipt by the office of the custodian may be deemed denied. The person requesting the public records may pursue the remedies provided in the Inspection of Public Records Act.

B. If a written request has been denied, the custodian shall provide the requester with a written explanation of the denial. The written denial shall:

   (1) describe the records sought;

   (2) set forth the names and titles or positions of each person responsible for the denial; and

   (3) be delivered or mailed to the person requesting the records within fifteen days after the request for inspection was received.

C. A custodian who does not deliver or mail a written explanation of denial within fifteen days after receipt of a written request for inspection is subject to an action to enforce the provisions of the Inspection of Public Records Act and the requester may be awarded damages. Damages shall:

(1) be awarded if the failure to provide a timely explanation of denial is determined to be unreasonable;

(2) not exceed one hundred dollars ($100) per day;

(3) accrue from the day the public body is in noncompliance until a written denial is issued; and

(4) be payable from the funds of the public body.

14-2-12. Enforcement.

A. An action to enforce the Inspection of Public Records Act may be brought by:

(1) the attorney general or the district attorney in the county of jurisdiction; or

(2) a person whose written request has been denied.

B. A district court may issue a writ of mandamus or order an injunction or other appropriate remedy to enforce the provisions of the Inspection of Public Records Act.

C. The exhaustion of administrative remedies shall not be required prior to bringing any action to enforce the procedures of the Inspection of Public Records Act.

D. The court shall award damages, costs and reasonable attorneys' fees to any person whose written request has been denied and is successful in a court action to enforce the provisions of the Inspection of Public Records Act.

APPENDIX II
IPRA GLOSSARY:
TERMS YOU NEED TO KNOW

Key IPRA Terms

Actual Damages - Real financial losses you can prove were caused by an IPRA violation. Unlike statutory damages, these require evidence of specific harm.

Burdensome Request - A records request that legitimately requires extra time beyond the standard 15-day deadline due to its size or complexity. Agencies must notify you in writing if they consider your request burdensome.

Custodian - The person designated by a public body to handle records requests. Every public agency must have at least one, and all IPRA lawsuits must name this person.

Deemed Denied - When an agency fails to respond to your request within 15 days (and hasn't designated it "burdensome"), your request is automatically considered denied, giving you the right to pursue legal action.

Electronic Format - Digital rather than paper records. If records exist electronically and you request them in that form, agencies must provide them electronically rather than printing them out.

Enforcement Action - A lawsuit filed in district court to force an agency to comply with IPRA. These actions can seek records, explanations for denials, and in some cases, damages.

Exemptions - Specific categories of records that agencies can legally withhold, such as certain law enforcement records or attorney-client communications. There are specific exceptions listed in IPRA plus any "otherwise provided by law."

Inspect - To view public records, either in person or by receiving copies. IPRA gives you the right to inspect records, not just receive summaries or answers to questions.

Metadata - "Data about data" - information that isn't visible in the document itself but describes its properties, such as when it was created, who created it, and how it's been modified.

Native Format - The original file format in which a record was created (like .docx for Word documents or .xlsx for Excel spreadsheets), rather than a converted format like PDF.

Otherwise Provided By Law - The catch-all exception referring to any records made confidential by other state or federal laws, court rules, or constitutional provisions.

Protected Personal Identifier Information - Specific personal details that agencies can redact, including social security numbers, all but the last 4 digits of financial account numbers, and non-business home addresses of non-elected employees.

Public Body - Any governmental entity subject to IPRA, including state agencies, local governments, school districts, and institutions receiving public funding.

Public Records - Any documents, regardless of format, that are created, used, maintained or held by a public body and relate to public business.

Reasonable Particularity - The required level of specificity in your request. You must describe records clearly enough that the agency can identify what you're seeking, though you don't need the exact document name or number.

Redaction - The process of removing or blacking out exempt information from records before releasing them.

Rolling Production - When an agency provides records in batches over time rather than all at once, usually for large requests.

Statutory Damages - Financial penalties of up to $100 per day that courts can award when an agency unreasonably fails to respond to a request or provide a proper explanation of denial.

Three-Day Letter - The acknowledgment an agency must send within three business days of receiving your request, explaining when records will be available or when they'll respond further.

Written Request - Any records request submitted in writing, including email, fax, or letter. Only written requests (not verbal ones) create legal obligations and can be enforced through court action.

Common Exceptions to Disclosure

Attorney-Client Privilege - Communications between a public body and its attorneys for the purpose of obtaining legal advice.

Confidential Materials Act - Allows libraries, museums, and similar institutions to keep confidential materials donated with access restrictions.

Law Enforcement Records - Certain law enforcement information is protected, particularly details about victims of specific crimes, visual depictions of death or great bodily harm, and confidential sources or methods.

Letters of Reference - Letters concerning employment, licensing or permits that give opinions about a person's qualifications.

Medical Records - Records pertaining to physical or mental examinations and medical treatment, particularly of persons confined to institutions.

Matters of Opinion - Letters or memos containing opinions (rather than facts) in personnel files or student files.

Trade Secrets - Confidential business information that has economic value from not being generally known and is subject to reasonable efforts to maintain secrecy.

Legal Terms You Might Encounter

Britton v. Office of the Attorney General - Important 2019 court decision establishing that incomplete responses (providing some but not all responsive records) may subject agencies to statutory damages.

Declaratory Judgment - A court ruling that officially establishes rights and duties between parties without ordering specific actions or awarding damages.

Faber v. King - Significant 2015 New Mexico Supreme Court case distinguishing between two types of IPRA damages and clarifying when each applies.

In Camera Review - When a judge privately examines records to determine if they're truly exempt from disclosure.

Injunction - A court order requiring an agency to take specific action, such as producing records.

Mandamus - A court order compelling a government official to properly fulfill their official duties, often used in IPRA cases to force production of records.

Republican Party of NM v. NM Taxation & Revenue Dept. - 2012 case that eliminated the "rule of reason" (a court-created IPRA exception) and limited executive privilege.

Standing - The legal right to bring a lawsuit. In IPRA cases, anyone whose written request has been denied has standing to sue.

Practical Terms for Records Management

Administrative Records - Documentation of day-to-day operations, such as correspondence, memoranda, and reports.

Archival Records - Records with long-term historical or legal value that are preserved permanently.

Disposition - What happens to records at the end of their retention period (destruction, permanent preservation, etc.).

Finding Aid - A document that helps locate specific information within a collection of records.

Record Series - A group of records organized by their function, subject, or activity.

Records Retention Schedule - An agency's formal policy detailing how long different types of records must be kept before disposal.

Responsive Records - Documents that contain the information requested in your IPRA request.

Withholding Log - A document listing records being withheld, the reason for withholding, and who made the decision.

Technical Terms for Electronic Records

Comma Separated Values (CSV) - A simple file format used to store tabular data that can be opened with spreadsheet programs or text editors.

Data Set - A collection of related data, often from a database, organized for analysis.

Electronic Discovery (E-Discovery) - The process of identifying and producing electronic information in legal proceedings.

Email Thread - A series of connected email messages that form a conversation between two or more people.

File Path - The location of a file within a computer's file system, showing the directories and subdirectories that contain it.

Optical Character Recognition (OCR) - Technology that converts images of text (like scanned documents) into machine-readable text that can be searched.

Portable Document Format (PDF) - A file format that preserves document formatting regardless of software, hardware, or operating system.

Structured Data - Information organized in a predefined way, typically in rows and columns, like databases and spreadsheets.

Unstructured Data - Information that doesn't have a predefined data model, such as emails, word processing documents, and social media posts.

Database-Specific Terms

Database - An organized collection of data stored electronically, typically designed for easy searching and retrieval.

Database Management System (DBMS) - Software that allows users to interact with a database to store, retrieve, and manipulate data.

Field - A single piece of information within a database record, like "last name" or "date of birth."

Query - A request for specific information from a database.

Record - A complete set of information about a specific item in a database, comprising multiple fields.

Report - A formatted presentation of database information, often designed for non-technical users.

Table - A collection of related data organized in rows and columns within a database.

Common Agency Abbreviations

AG - Attorney General

CABQ or **COA** - City of Albuquerque

CID - Construction Industries Division

COSF - City of Santa Fe

DFA - Department of Finance and Administration

DOH - Department of Health

DPS - Department of Public Safety

GSD - General Services Department

NMDOJ - New Mexico Department of Justice (formerly known as NMOAG or NMAGO, Office of the Attorney General)

NMED - New Mexico Environment Department

NMCD - New Mexico Corrections Department

PED - Public Education Department

RLD - Regulation and Licensing Department

TRD - Taxation and Revenue Department

APPENDIX III
RESOURCES FOR FEDERAL FOIA REQUESTS

Since this book focuses exclusively on New Mexico's IPRA, here are some resources for federal FOIA requests:

- FOIA.gov - The federal government's official FOIA website
- National Freedom of Information Coalition (NFOIC) – www. nfoic.org
- Reporters Committee for Freedom of the Press FOIA guides – www.rcfp.org/foia/
- MuckRock.com (platform for submitting and tracking FOIA requests)

APPENDIX IV
KEY NEW MEXICO DATABASES AND TRANSPARENCY PORTALS

Statewide Databases & Transparency Portals

New Mexico Sunshine Portal – https://ssp.nm.gov/

New Mexico Open Books Public Education Financial Transparency Portal – https://web.ped.nm.gov/open-books-public-education-financial-transparency-portal/

New Mexico Federal Funds Dashboards (NM DFA) – https://www.nmdfa.state.nm.us/dfa-dashboards/new-mexico-federal-funds-dashboards/

New Mexico Environment Department Open Data Portal – https://api.env.nm.gov/

Municipal & Local Government Transparency

City

City of Albuquerque ABQ Data – https://www.cabq.gov/abq-data

City of Albuquerque Inspector General – https://www.cabq.gov/inspectorgeneral

City of Santa Fe Sunshine Portal – https://santafenm.gov/city-clerk-1/sunshine-portal

County

County of Bernalillo Transparency Portal – https://www.bernco.gov/bernco-view/

County of Santa Fe Sunshine Portal – https://www.santafecountynm.gov/sunshine

McKinley County Transparency Portal – https://www.co.mckinley.nm.us/203/Transparency-Portal

Los Alamos County Financial Transparency / Open Books – https://www.losalamosnm.us/Government/Transparent-Los-Alamos-County/Financial-Transparency-Open-Books

Higher Education

University of New Mexico Sunshine Portal – https://sunshine.unm.edu/

Audit, Fiscal Oversight, & Legislative Transparency

New Mexico State Auditor Audit Report Search – https://www.osa.nm.gov/auditing/audit-report-search/

New Mexico State Auditor Transparency Reports – https://www.osa.nm.gov/accountability-office/transparency-reports/

New Mexico Legislative Finance Committee – https://www.nmlegis.gov/entity/lfc/Default

Public Records & Open Government Framework

Inspection of Public Records Act (IPRA) – https://nmdoj.gov/get-help/inspection-of-public-records-act/

Open Meetings Act Compliance Guide – https://www.nmag.gov/wp-content/uploads/Open-Meetings-Act-Compliance-Guide.pdf

505 Legal, PC

PO Box 90336

Albuquerque, NM 87199

(505) 421-3329

www.505legal.com